Travels through France and Italy. In two volumes. ... With a particular description of the town, territory, and climate of Nice. To which is added, a register of the weather, kept during a residence of eighteen months in that city Volume 1 of 2

Tobias George Smollett

Travels through France and Italy. In two volumes. ... With a particular description of the town, territory, and climate of Nice. To which is added, a register of the weather, kept during a residence of eighteen months in that city. By T. Smollett, M.D. .. Volume 1 of 2
Smollett, Tobias George
ESTCID: T055400
Reproduction from British Library

London : printed for R. Baldwin, 1778.
2v. ; 12°

Eighteenth Century
Collections Online
Print Editions

Gale ECCO Print Editions

Relive history with *Eighteenth Century Collections Online*, now available in print for the independent historian and collector. This series includes the most significant English-language and foreign-language works printed in Great Britain during the eighteenth century, and is organized in seven different subject areas including literature and language; medicine, science, and technology; and religion and philosophy. The collection also includes thousands of important works from the Americas.

The eighteenth century has been called "The Age of Enlightenment." It was a period of rapid advance in print culture and publishing, in world exploration, and in the rapid growth of science and technology – all of which had a profound impact on the political and cultural landscape. At the end of the century the American Revolution, French Revolution and Industrial Revolution, perhaps three of the most significant events in modern history, set in motion developments that eventually dominated world political, economic, and social life.

In a groundbreaking effort, Gale initiated a revolution of its own: digitization of epic proportions to preserve these invaluable works in the largest online archive of its kind. Contributions from major world libraries constitute over 175,000 original printed works. Scanned images of the actual pages, rather than transcriptions, recreate the works ***as they first appeared.***

Now for the first time, these high-quality digital scans of original works are available via print-on-demand, making them readily accessible to libraries, students, independent scholars, and readers of all ages.

For our initial release we have created seven robust collections to form one the world's most comprehensive catalogs of 18th century works.

Initial Gale ECCO Print Editions collections include:

History and Geography
Rich in titles on English life and social history, this collection spans the world as it was known to eighteenth-century historians and explorers. Titles include a wealth of travel accounts and diaries, histories of nations from throughout the world, and maps and charts of a world that was still being discovered. Students of the War of American Independence will find fascinating accounts from the British side of conflict.

Social Science
Delve into what it was like to live during the eighteenth century by reading the first-hand accounts of everyday people, including city dwellers and farmers, businessmen and bankers, artisans and merchants, artists and their patrons, politicians and their constituents. Original texts make the American, French, and Industrial revolutions vividly contemporary.

Medicine, Science and Technology
Medical theory and practice of the 1700s developed rapidly, as is evidenced by the extensive collection, which includes descriptions of diseases, their conditions, and treatments. Books on science and technology, agriculture, military technology, natural philosophy, even cookbooks, are all contained here.

Literature and Language
Western literary study flows out of eighteenth-century works by Alexander Pope, Daniel Defoe, Henry Fielding, Frances Burney, Denis Diderot, Johann Gottfried Herder, Johann Wolfgang von Goethe, and others. Experience the birth of the modern novel, or compare the development of language using dictionaries and grammar discourses.

Religion and Philosophy
The Age of Enlightenment profoundly enriched religious and philosophical understanding and continues to influence present-day thinking. Works collected here include masterpieces by David Hume, Immanuel Kant, and Jean-Jacques Rousseau, as well as religious sermons and moral debates on the issues of the day, such as the slave trade. The Age of Reason saw conflict between Protestantism and Catholicism transformed into one between faith and logic -- a debate that continues in the twenty-first century.

Law and Reference
This collection reveals the history of English common law and Empire law in a vastly changing world of British expansion. Dominating the legal field is the *Commentaries of the Law of England* by Sir William Blackstone, which first appeared in 1765. Reference works such as almanacs and catalogues continue to educate us by revealing the day-to-day workings of society.

Fine Arts
The eighteenth-century fascination with Greek and Roman antiquity followed the systematic excavation of the ruins at Pompeii and Herculaneum in southern Italy; and after 1750 a neoclassical style dominated all artistic fields. The titles here trace developments in mostly English-language works on painting, sculpture, architecture, music, theater, and other disciplines. Instructional works on musical instruments, catalogs of art objects, comic operas, and more are also included.

biblio life
old books. new life.

The BiblioLife Network

This project was made possible in part by the BiblioLife Network (BLN), a project aimed at addressing some of the huge challenges facing book preservationists around the world. The BLN includes libraries, library networks, archives, subject matter experts, online communities and library service providers. We believe every book ever published should be available as a high-quality print reproduction; printed on-demand anywhere in the world. This insures the ongoing accessibility of the content and helps generate sustainable revenue for the libraries and organizations that work to preserve these important materials.

The following book is in the "public domain" and represents an authentic reproduction of the text as printed by the original publisher. While we have attempted to accurately maintain the integrity of the original work, there are sometimes problems with the original work or the micro-film from which the books were digitized. This can result in minor errors in reproduction. Possible imperfections include missing and blurred pages, poor pictures, markings and other reproduction issues beyond our control. Because this work is culturally important, we have made it available as part of our commitment to protecting, preserving, and promoting the world's literature.

GUIDE TO FOLD-OUTS MAPS and OVERSIZED IMAGES

The book you are reading was digitized from microfilm captured over the past thirty to forty years. Years after the creation of the original microfilm, the book was converted to digital files and made available in an online database.

In an online database, page images do not need to conform to the size restrictions found in a printed book. When converting these images back into a printed bound book, the page sizes are standardized in ways that maintain the detail of the original. For large images, such as fold-out maps, the original page image is split into two or more pages

Guidelines used to determine how to split the page image follows:

- Some images are split vertically; large images require vertical and horizontal splits.
- For horizontal splits, the content is split left to right.
- For vertical splits, the content is split from top to bottom.
- For both vertical and horizontal splits, the image is processed from top left to bottom right.

TRAVELS
THROUGH
FRANCE AND ITALY.

IN TWO VOLUMES.

Containing OBSERVATIONS on

CHARACTER,	POLICE,
CUSTOMS,	COMMERCE,
RELIGION,	ARTS, and
GOVERNMENT,	ANTIQUITIES.

With a particular DESCRIPTION of the
TOWN, TERRITORY, AND CLIMATE OF NICE.

To which is added,
A REGISTER OF THE WEATHER,

Kept during a
Residence of Eighteen Months in that City.

BY T. SMOLLETT, M. D.

Ut homo qui erranti comiter monstrat viam,
Quasi lumen de suo lumine accendat, facit
Nihilominus ipse luceat, cum illi accenderit.   ENNIUS.

VOLUME THE FIRST.

LONDON:
Printed for R. BALDWIN, in Pater-noster-Row.

M.DCC.LXXVIII.

LETTER I.

Boulogne sur mer, June 23 1763.

DEAR SIR,

YOU laid your commands upon me at parting, to communicate, from time to time, the observations I should make in the course of my travels; and it was an injunction I received with pleasure. In gratifying your curiosity, I shall find some amusement to beguile the tedious hours, which, without some such employment, would be rendered insupportable by distemper and disquiet.

You knew and pitied my situation, traduced by malice, persecuted by faction, abandoned by false patrons, and overwhelmed by the sense of a domestic calamity, which it was not in the power of fortune to repair.

You know with what eagerness I fled from my country, as a scene of illiberal dispute and incredible infatuation, where a few worthless incendiaries had, by dint of perfidious calumnies and atrocious abuse, kindled up a flame which threatened all the horrors of civil dissension.

I packed up my little family in a hired coach; and, attended by my trusty servant, who had lived with me a dozen of years, and now refused to leave me, took the road to Dover, in my way to the South of France, where I hoped the mildness of the climate would prove favourable to the weak state of my lungs.

You advised me to have recourse again to the Bath-waters, from the use of which I had received great benefit the preceding winter. But I had many inducements to leave England. My wife earnestly begged I would convey her from a country where every object served to nourish her grief: I was in hopes that a succession of new scenes would engage her attention, and gradually call off her mind from a series of painful reflections; and I imagined the change of air, and a journey of near a thousand miles, would have a happy effect upon my own constitution. But as the summer was already advanced, and the heat too excessive for travelling in warm climates, I proposed staying at Boulogne till the beginning of autumn, and, in the mean time, to bathe in the sea, with a view to strengthen and prepare my body for the fatigues of such a long journey.

A man who travels with a family of five persons, must lay his account with a number of mortifications, and some of these I have already happily overcome. Though I was well acquainted with the road to Dover, and made allowances accordingly,

LETTER I.

I could not help being chagrined at the bad accommodation and impudent imposition to which I was exposed: these I found the more disagreeable, as we were detained a day extraordinary on the road, in consequence of my wife's being indisposed.

I need not tell you this is the worst road in England, with respect to the conveniences of travelling, and must certainly impress foreigners with an unfavourable opinion of the nation in general. The chambers are, in general, cold and comfortless, the beds paultry, the cookery execrable, the wine poison, the attendance bad, the publicans insolent, and the bills extortion: there is not a drop of tolerable malt liquor to be had from London to Dover.

Every landlord and every waiter harangued upon the knavery of a publican in Canterbury, who had charged the French ambassador forty pounds for a supper that was not worth forty shillings. They talked much of honesty and conscience; but when they produced their own bills, they appeared to be all of the same family and complexion. If it was a reproach upon the English nation that an inn-keeper should pillage strangers at that rate, it is a greater scandal that the same fellow should be able to keep his house still open. I own, I think it would be for the honour of the kingdom to reform the abuses of this road; and, in particular, to improve the avenue to London by the way of Kent-street, which is a most disgraceful entrance to such an opulent city. A foreigner, in passing through this beggarly and ruinous suburb, conceives such an idea of misery and meanness, as all the wealth and magnificence of London and Westminster are afterwards unable to destroy. A friend of mine, who brought a Parisian from Dover in his own post-chaise, contrived to enter Southwark after it was dark, that his friend might not perceive the nakedness of this quarter. The stranger was much pleased with the great number of shops full of merchandise, lighted up to the best advantage. He was astonished at the display of riches in Lombard-street and Cheapside. The badness of the pavement made him find the streets twice as long as they were. They alighted in Upper Brook-Street, by Grosvenor-Square; and when his conductor told him they were then about the middle of London, the Frenchman declared, with marks of infinite surprise, that London was very near as long as Paris.

On my arrival at Dover I paid off my coachman, who went away with a heavy heart: he wanted much to cross the sea, and endeavoured to persuade me to carry the coach and horses to the other side. If

LETTER I.

had been resolved to set out immediately for the South, perhaps I should have taken his advice. If I had retained him at the rate of twenty guineas per month, which was the price he demanded, and begun my journey without hesitation, I should travel more agreeably than I can expect to do in the carriages of this country, and the difference of the expence would be a mere trifle. I would advise every man who travels thro' France to bring his own vehicle along with him, or at least to purchase one at Calais or Boulogne, where second-hand berlins and chaises may be generally had at reasonable rates. I have been offered a very good berlin for thirty guineas; but before I make the purchase, I must be better informed touching the different methods of travelling in this country.

Dover is commonly termed a den of thieves; and I am afraid it is not altogether without reason it has acquired this appellation. The people are said to live by piracy in time of war, and by smuggling and fleecing strangers in time of peace; but I will do them the justice to say, they make no distinction between foreigners and natives. Without all doubt, a man cannot be much worse lodged and worse treated in any part of Europe; nor will he in any other place meet with more flagrant instances of fraud, imposition and brutality. One would imagine they had formed a general conspiracy against all those who either go to, or return from the continent. About five years ago, in my passage from Flushing to Dover, the master of the packet-boat brought to all of a sudden off the South Foreland, although the wind was as favourable as it could blow. He was immediately boarded by a custom-house boat, the officer of which appeared to be his friend: he then gave the passengers to understand, that as it was low water, the ship could not go into the harbour; but that the boat would carry them ashore with their baggage.

The custom-house officer demanded a guinea for this service, and the bargain was made. Before we quitted the ship, we were obliged to gratify the cabin-boy for his attendance, and to give drink-money to the sailors. The boat was run a-ground on the open beach; but we could not get ashore without the assistance of three or four fellows, who insisted upon being paid for their trouble. Every parcel and bundle, as it was landed, was snatched up by a separate porter: one ran away with a hat-box, another with a wig-box, a third with a couple of shirts tied up in a handkerchief, and two were employed in carrying a small portmanteau that did not weigh forty pounds. All our things were

LETTER I.

hurried to the custom-house to be searched, and the searcher was paid for disordering our cloaths; from thence they were removed to the inn, where the porters demanded half a crown each for their labour. It was in vain to expostulate; they surrounded the house like a pack of hungry hounds, and raised such a clamour, that we were fain to comply. After we had undergone all this imposition, we were visited by the master of the packet, who having taken our fares, and wished us joy of our happy arrival in England, expressed his hope that we would remember the poor master, whose wages were very small, and who chiefly depended on the generosity of passengers. I own I was shocked at his meanness, and could not help telling him so. I told him, I could not conceive what title he had to any such gratification: he had sixteen passengers, who paid a guinea each, on the supposition that every person should have a bed; but there were no more than eight beds in the cabin, and each of these was occupied before I came on board; so that if we had been detained at sea a whole week by contrary winds and bad weather, one half of the passengers must have sleeped upon the boards, howsoever their health might have suffered from this want of accommodation. Notwithstanding this check, he was so very abject and importunate, that we gave him a crown a-piece, and he retired.

The first thing I did when I arrived at Dover this last time, was to send for the master of a packet-boat, and agree with him to carry us to Boulogne at once, by which means I saved the expence of travelling by land from Calais to this last place, a journey of four-and-twenty miles. The hire of a vessel from Dover to Boulogne is precisely the same as from Dover to Calais, five guineas; but this skipper demanded eight, and, as I did not know the fare I agreed to give him six. We embarked between six and seven in the evening, and found ourselves in a most wretched hovel, on board what is called *a Folkstone cutter*. The cabin was so small, that a dog could hardly turn in it, and the beds put me in mind of the holes described in some catacombs, in which the bodies of the dead were deposited, being thrust in with the feet foremost; there was no getting into them but end-ways, and indeed they seemed so dirty that nothing but extreme necessity could have obilged me to use them. We sat up all night in a most uncomfortable situation, tossed about by the sea, cold and cramped and weary, and languishing for want of sleep. At three in the morning the master came down, and told us we were just off the harbour of Boulogne; but the wind blowing off shore, he could not possibly enter, and therefore advised us to go ashore in the boat. I went upon deck to view the coast, when he pointed to the place where he said Boulogne stood, declaring, at the same time, we were within a short mile of the harbour's mouth. The morning was cold and raw, and I knew myself extremely subject to catch cold; nevertheless, we were all so impatient to be ashore, that I resolved to take his advice. The boat was already hoisted out, and we went on board of it, after I had paid the captain, and gratified his crew. We had scarce parted from the ship, when we perceived a boat coming towards us from the shore; and the master gave us to understand, it was coming to carry us into the harbour. When I objected to the trouble of shifting from one boat to another in the open sea, which (by the bye) was a little rough; he said it was a privilege which the watermen of Boulogne had, to carry all passengers ashore, and that this privilege he durst not venture to infringe. This was no time nor place to remonstrate. The French boat came along side half filled with water, and we were handed from the one to the other. We were then obliged to lye upon our oars, till the captain's boat went on board and returned from the ship with a packet of letters. We were afterwards rowed a long league, in a rough sea, against wind and tide, before we reached the harbour, where we landed, benumbed with cold, and the women excessively sick: from our landing-place we were obliged to walk very near a mile to the inn where we purposed to lodge, attended by six or seven men and women, bare-legged, carrying our baggage. This boat cost me a guinea, besides paying exorbitantly the people who carried our things; so that the inhabitants of Dover and of Boulogne seem to be of the same kidney, and indeed they understand one another perfectly well. It was our honest captain who made the signal for the shore-boat before I went upon deck; by which means he not only gratified his friends, the watermen of Boulogne, but also saved about fifteen shillings portage, which he must have paid had he gone into the harbour; and thus he found himself at liberty to return to Dover, which he reached in four hours. I mention these circumstances as a warning to other passengers. When a man hires a packet-boat from Dover to Calais or Boulogne, let him remember that the stated price is five guineas; and let him insist upon being carried into the harbour in the ship, without paying the least regard to the representations of the master, who is generally a little dirty knave. When he tells you it is low water, or the wind is in your teeth, you may say you will stay on board till it is high water, or till the wind comes favourable. If he sees you are resolute, he will find means to bring his ship into the harbour, or at least to convince you, without a possibility of your being deceived, that it is not in his power. After all, the fellow himself was a loser by his finesse; if he had gone into the harbour, he would have had another fare immediately back to Dover, for there was a Scotch gentleman at the inn waiting for such an opportunity.

Knowing my own weak constitution, I took it for granted this morning's adventure would cost me a fit of illness; and what added to my chagrin, when we arrived at the inn, all the beds were occupied; so that we were obliged to sit in a cold kitchen above two hours, until some of the lodgers should get up. This was such a bad specimen of French accommodation, that my wife could not help regretting even the inns of Rochester, Sittingbourn, and Canterbury. bad as they are, they certainly have the advantage, when compared with the execrable auburges of this country, where one finds nothing but dirt and imposition. One would imagine in a ship from the river Thames, I underwent this ordeal. But what gives me more vexation, my books have been stopped at the bureau; and will be sent to Amiens at my expence, to be examined by the *chambre syndicale*, left they should contain something prejudicial to the state, or to the religion of the country. This is a species of oppression which one would not expect to meet with in France, which piques itself on its politeness and hospitality: but the truth is, I know no country in which strangers are worse treated, with respect to their essential concerns. If a foreigner dies in France, the king seizes all his effects, even though his heir should be upon the spot; and this tyrrany is called the *droit d' aubaine*, founded at first upon the supposition that all the estate of foreigners residing in France was acquired in that kingdom, and that therefore it would be unjust to convey it to another country. If an English Protestant goes to France for the benefit of his health, attended by his wife or his son, or both, and dies with effects in the house to the amount of a thousand guineas, the king seizes the whole, the family is left destitute, and the body of the deceased is denied Christian burial. The Swiss, by capitulation, are exempted from this despotism, and so are the Scots, in consequence of an ancient alliance between the two nations. The same *droit d' aubaine* is exacted by some of the princes in Germany: but it is a great discouragement to commerce, and prejudices every country where it is exercised, to ten times the value of what it brings into the coffers of the sovereign.

I am exceedingly mortified at the detention of my books, which not only deprives me of an amusement which I can very ill dispense with, but, in all probability, will expose me to sundry other inconveniencies. I must be at the expence of sending them sixty miles to be examined, and run the risque of their being condemned: and, in the mean time, I may lose the opportunity of sending them with my heavy baggage by sea to Bourdeaux, to be sent up the Garonne to Tholouse, and from thence transmitted through the canal of Languedoc to Cette, which is a sea-port on the Mediterranean, about three or four leagues from Montpelier.

For the recovery of my books, I had recourse to the advice of my landlord, Monsf. B——. He is a handsome young fellow, about twenty-five years of age, and keeps house with two maiden sisters, who are professed devotees. The brother is a little libertine, good natured and obliging; but a true Frenchman in vanity, which is undoubtedly the ruling passion of this volatile people. He has an inconsiderable place under the government, in consequence of which he is permitted to wear a sword, a privilege which he does not fail to use. He is likewise receiver of the tythes of the clergy in this district, an office that gives him a command of money; and he, moreover, deals in the wine trade. When I came to his house, he made a parade of all these advantages: he displayed his bags of money, and some old gold which his father had left him. He described his chateau in the country: dropped hints of the fortunes that were settled upon mademoiselles his sisters; boasted of his connections at court; and assured me it was not for my money that he let his lodgings, but altogether with a view to enjoy the pleasure of my company. The truth, when stripped of all embellishments, is this: the sieur B—— is the son of an honest bourgeois lately dead, who left him the house, with some stock in trade, a little money, and a paltry farm; his sisters have about three thousand livres (not quite 140 l.) a-piece; the brother's places are worth about fifty pounds a-year, and his connections at court are confined to a commis or clerk in the secretary's office, with whom he corresponds by virtue of his employment. My landlord piques himself upon his gallantry and succefs with the fair fex: he keeps a *fille de joye*, and makes no fecret of his amours. He told Mifs C—— the other day, in broken Englifh, that, in the courfe of the laft year, he had made fix baftards. He owned, at the fame time, he had fent them all to the hofpital; but, now his father is dead, he would himfelf take care of his future productions. This, however, was no better than a gafconade.—Yefterday the houfe was in a hot alarm, on account of a new windfall of this kind: the fifters were in tears; the brother was vifited by the *cure* of the parifh; the lady in the ftraw (a fempftrefs) fent him the bantling in a bafket, and he tranfmitted it by the carriers to the *Enfans trouves* at Paris.

But to return from this digreffion: Mr B—— advifed me to fend a *requete* or petition to the chancellor of France, that I might obtain an order to have my books examined on the fpot, by the prefident of Boulogne, or the *procureur du roy*, or the fub-delegate of the intendance. He recommended an *avocat* of his acquaintance to draw up the *memoire*, and introduced him accordingly; telling me at the fame time, in private, that if he was not a drunkard, he would be at the head of his profeffion. He had indeed all the outward figns of a fot; a fleepy eye, a rubicund face, and carbuncled nose. He seemed to be a little out at elbows, had marvellous foul linen, and his breeches were not very sound: but he assumed an air of importance, was very courteous, and very solemn. I asked him if he did not sometimes divert himself with the muse: he smiled, and promised, in a whisper, to show me some *chansonettes de sa facon*. Meanwhile he composed the *requete* in my name, which was very pompous, very tedious, and very abject. Such a style might perhaps be necessary in a native of France; but I did not think it was at all suitable to a subject of Great Britain. I thanked him for the trouble he had taken, as he would receive no other gratification: but when my landlord proposed to send the *memoire* to his correspondent at Paris, to be delivered to the chancellor, I told him I had changed my mind, and would apply to the English ambassador. I have accordingly taken the liberty to address myself to the Earl of H——; and at the same time I have presumed to write to the Duchess of D——, who is now at Paris, to intreat her Grace's advice and interposition. What effect these applications may have, I know not: but the sieur B—— shakes his head, and has told my servant, in confidence, that I am mistaken if I think the English ambassador is as great a man at Paris as the chancellor of France.

I ought to make an apology for troubling you with such an unentertaining detail, and consider that the detention of my books must be a matter of very little consequence to any body, but to

Your affectionate humble servant.

LETTER III.

Boulogne, August 15, 1763

SIR,

I Am much obliged to you for your kind inquiries after my health, which has been lately in a very declining condition. In consequence of a cold, caught a few days after my arrival in France, I was seized with a violent cough, attended with a fever, and stitches in my breast, which tormented me all night long without ceasing. At the same time I had a great discharge by expectoration, and such a dejection of spirits as I never felt before. In this situation I took a step which may appear to have been desperate. I knew there was no imposthume in my lungs, and I supposed the stitches were spasmodical. I was sensible that all my complaints were originally derived from relaxation. I therefore hired a chaise, and going to the beach, about a league from the town, plunged into the sea without hesitation. By this desperate remedy, I got a fresh cold in my head: but my stitches and fever vanished the very first day; and by a daily repetition of the bath, I have diminished my cough, strengthened my body, and recovered my spirits. I believe I should have tried the same experiment, even if there had been an abscess in my lungs, though such practice would have been contrary to all the rules of medicine but I am not one of those who implicitly believe in all the dogmata of physic. I saw one of the guides at Bath, the stoutest fellow among them, who recovered from the last stage of a consumption, by going into the king's bath, contrary to the express injunction of his doctor. He said, if he must die, the sooner the better, as he had nothing left for his subsistence. Instead of immediate death, he found instant ease, and continued mending every day, till his health was entirely re-established. I myself drank the waters at Bath, and bathed, in diametrical opposition to the opinion of some physicians there settled, and found myself better every day, notwithstanding their unfavourable prognostic. If I had been of the rigid fibre, full of blood, subject to inflammation, I should have followed a different course. Our acquaintance, doctor C——, while he actually spit up matter, and rode out every day for his life, led his horse to water, at the pond in Hyde-park, one cold frosty morning; and the beast, which happened to be of a hot constitution, plunged himself and his master over head and ears in the water. The poor doctor hastened home, half dead with fear, and was put to bed in the apprehension of a new imposthume; instead of which, he found himself exceedingly recruited in his spirits, and his appetite much mended. I advised him to take the hint, and go into the cold bath every morning: but he did not chuse to run any risque. How cold water comes to be such a bugbear, I know not, if I am not mistaken, Hippocrates recommends immersion in cold water for the gout; and Celsus expressly says, *in omni tussi utilis est natatio*.

I have conversed with a physician of this place, a sensible man, who assured me he was reduced to mere skin and bone by a cough and hectic fever, when he ordered a bath to be made in his own house, and dipped himself in cold water every morning. He at the same time left off drinking and swallowing any liquid that was warm. He is now strong and lusty, and even in winter has no other cover than a single sheet. His notions about the warm drink were a little whimsical: he imagined it relaxed the tone of the stomach; and this would undoubtedly be the case if it was drank in large quantities, warmer than the natural temperature of the blood. He alledged the example of the inhabitants of the Ladrone islands, who never taste any thing that is not cold, and are remarkably healthy. But to balance this argument I mentioned the Chinese, who scarce drink any thing but warm tea; and the Laplanders, who drink nothing but warm water; yet the people of both these nations are remarkably strong, healthy, and long-lived.

You desire to know the fate of my books. My Lord H―――d is not yet come to France; but my letter was transmitted to him from Paris: and his Lordship, with that generous humanity which is peculiar to his character, has done me the honour to assure me, under his own hand, that he has directed Mr N――lle, our resident at Paris, to apply for an order that my books may be restored.

I have met with another piece of good fortune, in being introduced to General Paterson and his lady, in their way to England from Nice, where the General has been many years commandant for the King of Sardinia. You must have heard of this gentleman, who has not only eminently distinguished himself, by his courage and conduct as an officer; but also by his probity and humanity in the exercise of his office, and by his remarkable hospitality to all strangers, especially the subjects of Great Britain, whose occasions called them to the place where he commanded. Being pretty far advanced in years, he begged leave to resign, that he might spend the evening of his days in his own country; and his Sardinian majesty granted his request with regret, after having honoured him with very particular marks of approbation and esteem. The General talks so favourably of the climate of Nice, with respect to disorders of the breast, that I am now determined to go thither. It would have been happy for me had he continued in his government. I think myself still very fortunate, in having obtained of him a letter of recommendation to the English consul of Nice, together with directions how to travel through the South of France. I propose to begin my journey some time next month when the weather will be temperate to the southward; and in the wine countries I shall have the pleasure of seeing the vintage, which is always a season of festivity among all ranks of people.

You have been very much mis-informed by the person who compared Boulogne to Wapping; he did a manifest injustice to this place, which is a large agreeable town, with broad open streets, excellently paved; and the houses are of stone, well built and commodious. The number of inhabitants may amount to sixteen thousand. You know this was generally supposed to be the *portus Itius*, and *Gessoriacum* of the ancients: though it is now believed that the *portus Itius*, from whence Cæsar sailed to Britain, is a place called *Whitsand*, about half way between this place and Calais. Boulogne is the capital of the Boulonnois, a district extending about twelve leagues, ruled by a governor independent of the governor of Piccardy; of which province, however, this country forms a part. The present governor is the duc d'Aumont. The town of Boulogne is the see of a bishop suffragan of Rheims, whose revenue amounts to about four and twenty thousand livres, or one thousand pounds sterling. It is also the seat of a seneschal's court, from whence an appeal lyes to the parliament of Paris; and thither all condemned criminals are sent, to have their sentence confirmed or reversed. Here is likewise a bailiwick, and a court of admiralty. The military jurisdiction of the city belongs to a commandant appointed by the king, a sort of sinecure bestowed upon some old officer. His appointments are very inconsiderable:

he resides in the Upper Town, and his garrison at present consists of a few hundreds of invalids.

Boulogne is divided into the Upper and Lower Towns. The former is a kind of citadel, about a short mile in circumference, situated on a rising ground, surrounded by a high wall and rampart, planted with rows of trees, which form a delightful walk. It commands a fine view of the country and Lower Town; and in clear weather the coast of England, from Dover to Folkstone, appears so plain, that one would imagine it was within four or five leagues of the French shore. The Upper Town was formerly fortified with outworks, which are now in ruins. Here is a square, a town house, a cathedral, and two or three convents of nuns; in one of which there are several English girls, sent hither for their education. The smallness of the expence encourages parents to send their children abroad to these seminaries, where they learn scarce any thing that is useful, but the French language; but they never fail to imbibe prejudices against the Protestant religion, and generally return enthusiastic converts to the religion of Rome. This conversion always generates a contempt for, and often an aversion to, their own country. Indeed it cannot reasonably be expected that people of weak minds, addicted to superstition, should either love or esteem those whom they are taught to consider as reprobated heretics. Ten pounds a year is the usual pension in these convents; but I have been informed by a French lady, who had her education in one of them, that nothing can be more wretched than their entertainment.

The civil magistracy of Boulogne consists of a mayor and echevins; and this is the case in almost all the towns of France.

The Lower Town is continued from the gate of the Upper Town, down the slope of a hill, as far as the harbour, stretching on both sides to a large extent, and is much more considerable than the Upper, with respect to the beauty of the streets, the convenience of the houses, and the number and wealth of the inhabitants. These, however, are all merchants, or bourgeois; for the noblesse or gentry live all together in the Upper Town, and never mix with the others. The harbour of Boulogne is at the mouth of the small river, or rather rivulet Liane, which is so shallow that the children wade through it at low water. As the tide makes, the sea flows in, and forms a pretty extensive harbour, which, however, admits nothing but small vessels. It is contracted at the mouth by two stone *jetties* or piers, which seem to have been constructed by some engineer very little acquainted with this branch of his profession; for they are carried out in such a manner, as to collect a bank of sand just at the entrance of the harbour. The road is very open and unsafe, and the surf very high when the wind blows from the sea. There is no fortification near the harbour, except a paltry fort mounting about twenty guns, built in the last war by the prince de Cruy, upon a rock about a league to the eastward of Boulogne. It appears to be situated in such a manner, that it can neither offend, nor be offended. If the depth of water would admit a forty or fifty gun ship to lye within cannon-shot of it, I apprehend it might be silenced in half an hour; but, in all probability, there will be no vestiges of it at the next rupture between the two crowns. It is surrounded every day by the sea at high water; and when it blows a fresh gale towards the shore, the waves break over the top of it, to the terror and astonishment of the garrison, who have been often heard crying piteously for assistance. I am persuaded that it will one day disappear in the twinkling of an eye. The neighbourhood of this fort, which is a smooth sandy beach, I have chosen for my bathing place. The road to it is agreeable and romantic, lying through pleasant corn-fields, skirted by open downs, where there is a rabbit warren, and great plenty of the birds so much admired at Tunbridge under the name of *white ears*. By the bye, this is a pleasant corruption of *white a—se*, the translation of their French name *cul blank*, taken from their colour; for they are actually white towards the tail.

Upon the top of a high rock, which overlooks the harbour, are the remains of an old fortification, which is indiscriminately called, *Tour d'ordre*, and *Julius Cæsar's fort*. The original tower was a light house built by *Claudius Cæsar*, denominated *Turris ardens*, from the fire burned in it; and this the French have corrupted into *Tour d'ordre:* but no vestiges of this Roman work remain; what we now see, are the ruins of a castle built by Charlemagne. I know of no other antiquity at Boulogne, except an old vault in the Upper Town, now used as a magazine, which is said to be part of an ancient temple dedicated to Isis.

On the other side of the harbour, opposite to the Lower Town, there is a house built, at a considerable expence, by a general officer, who lost his life in the late war. Never was situation more inconvenient, unpleasant, and unhealthy. It stands on the edge of an ugly morass, formed by the stagnant water left by the tide in its retreat. the very walks of the garden are so moist, that, in the driest weather, no person can make a tour of it without danger of the rheumatism. Besides, the house is altogether inaccessible except at low water, and even then the carriage must cross the harbour, the wheels up to the axle-tree in mud: nay, the tide rushes in so fast, that unless you seize the time to a minute, you will be in danger of perishing. The apartments of this house are elegantly fitted up, but very small; and the garden, notwithstanding its unfavourable situation, affords a great quantity of good fruit. The ooze, impregnated with sea salt, produces, on this side of the harbour, an incredible quantity of the finest *samphire* I ever saw. The French call it *passe-pierre*, and I suspect its English name is a corruption of *sang-pierre*. It is generally found on the faces of bare rocks that overhang the sea, by the spray of which it is nourished. As it grew upon a naked rock without any appearance of soil, it might be naturally enough called *sang du pierre*, or *sang-pierre*, blood of the rock; and hence the name *samphire*. On the same side of the harbour there is another new house, neatly built, belonging to a gentleman who has obtained a grant from the king of some ground which was always overflowed at high water. He has raised dykes at a considerable expence, to exclude the tide; and if he can bring his project to bear, he will not only gain a good estate for himself, but also improve the harbour, by increasing the depth at high water.

In the Lower Town of Boulogne there are several religious houses, particularly a seminary, a convent of Cordeliers, and another of Capuchins. This last having fallen to decay, was some years ago repaired, chiefly by the charity of British travellers, collected by father Græme, a native of North-Britain, who had been an officer in the army of King James II. and is said to have turned monk of this mendicant order, by way of voluntary penance for having killed his friend in a duel. Be that as it may, he was a well-bred, sensible man, of a very exemplary life and conversation; and his memory is much revered in this place. Being Superior of the convent, he caused the British arms to be put up in the church, as a mark of gratitude for the benefactions received from our nation. I often walk in the garden of the convent, the walls of which are washed by the sea at high water. At the bottom of the garden is a little private grove, separated from it by a high wall, with a door of communication, and hither the Capuchins retire, when they are disposed for contemplation.

LETTER III.

About two years ago, this place was said to be converted to a very different use. There was among the monks one *pere Charles*, a lusty friar, of whom the people tell strange stories. Some young women of the town were seen mounting over the wall by a ladder of ropes, in the dusk of the evening; and there was an unusual crop of bastards that season. In short, *pere Charles* and his companions gave such scandal, that the whole fraternity was changed; and now the nest is occupied by another flight of these birds of passage. If one of our privateers had kidnapped a Capuchin during the war and exhibited him in his habit, as a shew in London, he would have proved a good prize to the captors; for I know not a more uncouth and grotesque animal, than an old Capuchin in the habit of his order. A friend of mine, (a Swiss officer) told me, that a peasant in his country used to weep bitterly whenever a certain Capuchin mounted the pulpit to hold forth to the people. The good father took notice of this man, and believed he was touched by the finger of the Lord: he exhorted him to encourage these accessions of grace, and, at the same time, to be of good comfort, as having received such marks of the divine favour. The man still continued to weep as before, every time the monk preached; and at last the Capuchin insisted upon knowing what it was in his discourse or appearance, that made such an impression upon his heart.—" Ah, father! (cried "the peasant) I never see you but I think "of a venerable goat which I lost at East- "er: we were bred up together in the "same family: he was the very picture "of your reverence—one would swear you "were brothers. Poor *Baudouin!* he died "of a fall——rest his soul! I would will- "ingly pay for a couple of masses to pray "him out of purgatory."

Among other public edifices at Boulogne, there is an hospital or workhouse, which seems to be established upon a very good foundation. It maintains several hundreds of poor people, who are kept constantly at work, according to their age and abilities, in making thread, all sorts of lace, a kind of catgut, and in knitting stockings. It is under the direction of a bishop, and the see is at present filled by a prelate of great piety and benevolence, tho' a little inclining to bigotry and fanaticism. The churches in this town are but indifferently built, and poorly ornamented: there is not one picture in the place worth looking at, nor indeed does there seem to be the least taste for the liberal arts.

In my next, I shall endeavour to satisfy you in the other articles you desire to know. Mean-while, I am ever

Yours.

LETTER IV.

Boulogne, September 1. 1763.

SIR,

I Am infinitely obliged to D. H—— for the favourable manner in which he has mentioned me to the Earl of H——. I have at laſt recovered my books, by virtue of a particular order to the director of the douane, procured by the application of the Engliſh reſident to the French miniſtry. I am now preparing for my long journey; but before I leave this place, I ſhall ſend you the packet I mentioned, by Meriton. Mean-while I muſt fulfil my promiſe, in communicating the obſervations I have had occaſion to make upon this town and country.

The air of Boulogne is cold and moiſt, and, I believe, of conſequence unhealthy. Laſt winter the froſt, which continued ſix weeks in London, laſted here eight weeks without intermiſſion; and the cold was ſo intenſe, that, in the garden of the Capuchins, it ſplit the bark of ſeveral elms from top to bottom. On our arrival here we found all kinds of fruit more backward than in England. The froſt, in its progreſs in its progress to Britain, is much weakened in crossing the sea. The atmosphere impregnated with saline particles, resists the operation of freezing. Hence, in severe winters, all places near the sea-side are less cold than more inland districts. This is the reason why the winter is often more mild at Edinburgh than at London. A very great degree of cold is required to freeze salt water. Indeed it will not freeze at all, until it has deposited all its salt. It is now generally allowed among philosophers that water is no more than ice thawed by heat, either solar or subterranean, or both; and that this heat being expelled, it would return to its natural consistence. This being the case, nothing else is required for the freezing of water, than a certain degree of cold, which may be generated by the help of salt, or spirit of nitre, even under the line. I would propose, therefore, that an apparatus of this sort should be provided in every ship that goes to sea; and in case there should be a deficiency of fresh water on board, the sea water may be rendered potable, by being first converted into ice.

The air of Boulogne is not only loaded with a great evaporation from the sea, increased by strong gales of wind from the west and south-west, which blow almost continually during the greatest part of the year; but it is also subject to putrid vapours, arising from the low marshy ground in the neighbourhood of the harbour, which is every tide overflowed with sea-water. This may be one cause of the scrofula and rickets, which are two prevailing disorders among the children in Boulogne; but I believe the former is more owing to the water used in the Lower Town, which is very hard and unwholesome: it curdles with soap, gives a red colour to the meat that is boiled in it, and, when drank by strangers, never fails to occasion pains in the stomach and bowels; nay, sometimes produces dysenteries. In all appearance it is impregnated with nitre, if not with something more mischievous. We know that mundic, or pyrites, very often contains a proportion of arsenic, mixed with sulphur, vitriol, and mercury. Perhaps it partakes of the acid of some coal mine; for there are coal-works in this district. There is a well of purging water within a quarter of a mile of the Upper Town, to which the inhabitants resort in the morning, as the people of London go to the Dog-and-duck, in St. George's fields. There is likewise a fountain of excellent water, hard by the cathedral in the Upper Town, from whence I am daily supplied at a small expence. Some modern chemists affirm, that no saline chalybeate waters can exist, except in the neighbourhood of coal-damps; and that nothing can be more mild and gentle, and friendly to the constitution, than the said damps: but I know that the place where I was bred stands upon a zonic of coal; that the water which the inhabitants generally use is hard and brackish; and that the people are remarkably subject to the king's evil and consumption. These I would impute to the bad water, impregnated with the vitriol and brine of coal, as there is nothing in the constitution of the air that should render such distempers endemial. That the air of Boulogne encourages putrefaction, appears from the effect it has upon butcher's meat, which, though the season is remarkably cold, we can hardly keep four-and-twenty hours in the coolest part of the house.

Living here is pretty reasonable; and the markets are tolerably supplied. The beef is neither fat nor firm; but very good for soup, which is the only use the French make of it. The veal is not so white, nor so well fed, as the English veal; but it is more juicy, and better tasted. The mutton and pork are very good. We buy our poultry alive, and fatten them at home. Here are excellent turkies, and no want of game: the hares, in particular, are very large, juicy, and high flavoured. The best part of the fish caught on this coast is sent post to Paris, in chasse-marines, by a company of contractors, like those of Hastings in Sussex. Nevertheless, we have excellent soles, skaite, flounders and whitings, and sometimes mackarel. The oysters are very large, coarse, and rank. There is very little fish caught on the French coast, because the shallows run a great way from the shore; and the fish live chiefly in deep water: for this reason the fishermen go a a great way out to sea, sometimes even as far as the coast of England. Notwithstanding all the haste the contractors can make, their fish in the summer is very often spoiled before it arrives at Paris; and this is not to be wondered at, considering the length of the way, which is near one hundred and fifty miles. At best it must be in such a mortified condition, that no other people, except the negroes on the coast of Guinea, would feed upon it.

The wine commonly drank at Boulogne comes from Auxerre, is very small and meagre, and may be had from five to eight sols a bottle; that is from twopence halfpenny to fourpence. The French inhabitants drink no good wine; nor is there any to be had, unless you have recourse to the British wine-merchants here established, who deal in Bourdeaux wines, brought hither by sea for the London market. I have very good claret from a friend, at the rate of fifteenpence sterling a bottle; and excellent small beer as reasonable as in England. I don't believe there is a drop of generous Burgundy in the place; and the aubergistes impose upon us shamefully, when they charge it at two livres a bottle. There is a small white wine, called *preniac*, which is very agreeable, and very cheap. All the brandy which I have seen in Boulogne is new, fiery, and still burnt. This is the trash which smugglers import into Englnd. they have it for about tenpence a gallon. Butchers meat is sold for five sols, or twopence halfpenny a pound, and the pound here consists of eighteen ounces. I have a young turkey for thirty sols; a hare for four-and-twenty; a couple of chickens for twenty sols, and a couple of good soles for the same price. Before we left England, we were told that there was no fruit in Boulogne; but we have found ourselves agreeably disappointed in this particular. The place is well supplied with strawberries, cherries, gooseberries, corinths, peaches, apricots, and excellent pears. I have eaten more fruit this season, than I have done for several years. There are many well-cultivated gardens in the skirts of the town; particularly one belonging to our friend Mrs B--, where we often drank tea in a charming summer-house built on a rising ground, which commands a delightful prospect of the sea. We have many obligations to this good la-

LETTER IV.

dy, who is a kind neighbour, an obliging friend, and a most agreeable companion: she speaks English prettily, and is greatly attached to the people and customs of our nation. They use wood for their common fewel, tho', if I were to live at Boulogne, I would mix it with coal, which this country affords. Both the wood and the coal are reasonable enough. I am certain that a man may keep house in Boulogne for about one half of what it will cost him in London; and this is said to be one of the dearest places in France.

The adjacent country is very agreeable, diversified with hill and dale, corn-fields, woods, and meadows. There is a forest of a considerable extent, that begins about a short league from the Upper Town: it belongs to the king, and the wood is farmed to different individuals.

In point of agriculture, the people in this neighbourhood seem to have profited by the example of the English. Since I was last in France, fifteen years ago, a good number of inclosures and plantations have been made in the English fashion. There is a good many tolerable country-houses within a few miles of Boulogne, but mostly empty. I was offered a complete house, with a garden of four acres well laid out, and two fields for grass or hay, about a mile from the town, for four hundred livres, about seventeen pounds a year; it is partly furnished, stands in an agreeable situation, with a fine prospect of the sea, and was lately occupied by a Scotch nobleman, who is in the service of France.

To judge from appearance, the people of Boulogne are descended from the Flemings, who formerly possessed this country; for a great many of the present inhabitants have fine skins, fair hair, and florid complexions; very different from the natives of France in general, who are distinguished by black hair, brown skins, and swarthy faces. The people of the Boulonnois enjoy some extraordinary privileges, and, in particular, are exempted from the gabelle or duties upon salt. How they deserved this mark of favour, I do not know; but they seem to have a spirit of independence among them, are very ferocious, and much addicted to revenge. Many barbarous murders are committed, both in the town and country; and the peasants, from motives of envy and resentment, frequently set their neighbours houses on fire. Several instances of this kind have happened in the course of the last year. The interruption which is given, in arbitrary governments, to the administration of justice, by the interposition of the great, has always a bad effect upon the morals of the common people. The peasants too are often rendered desperate and savage, by the misery they suffer from the oppression and tyranny of their landlords. In this neighbourhood the labouring people are ill lodged and wretchedly fed; and they have no idea of cleanliness. There is a substantial burgher in the High Town, who was some years ago convicted of a most barbarous murder. He received sentence to be broke alive upon the wheel; but was pardoned by the interposition of the governor of the county, and carries on his business as usual in the face of the whole community. A furious *abbe*, being refused orders by the bishop, on account of his irregular life, took an opportunity to stab the prelate with a knife, one Sunday, as he walked out of the cathedral. The good bishop desired he might be permitted to escape; but it was thought proper to punish with the utmost severity, such an atrocious attempt. He was accordingly apprehended, and, though the wound was not mortal, condemned to be broke. When this dreadful sentence was executed, he cried out, that it was hard he should undergo such torments, for having wounded a worthless priest, by whom he had been injured, while such a one (naming the burgher mentioned above) lived in ease and security, after having brutally murdered a poor man, and a helpless woman big with child, who had not given him the least provocation.

LETTER IV.

The inhabitants of Boulogne may be divided into three classes; the noblesse or gentry, the burghers, and the canaille. I don't mention the clergy, and the people belonging to the law, because I shall occasionally trouble you with my thoughts upon the religion and ecclesiastics of this country: and as for the lawyers, exclusive of their profession, they may be considered as belonging to one or other of these divisions. The noblesse are vain, proud, poor and slothful. Very few of them have above six thousand livres a year, which may amount to about two hundred and fifty pounds sterling; and many of them have not half this revenue. I think there is one heiress, said to be worth one hundred thousand livres, about four thousand two hundred pounds; but then her jewels, her cloaths, and even her linen, are reckoned part of this fortune. The noblesse have not the common sense to reside at their houses in the country, where, by farming their own grounds, they might live at a small expence, and improve their estates at the same time. They allow their country-houses to go to decay, and their gardens and fields to waste, and reside in dark holes in the Upper Town of Boulogne, without light, air, or convenience. There they starve within doors, that they may have wherewithal to purchase fine cloaths, and appear dressed once a day

LETTER IV.

in the church, or on the rampart. They have no education, no taste for reading, no housewifery, nor indeed any earthly occupation, but that of dressing their hair, and adorning their bodies. They hate walking, and would never go abroad, if they were not stimulated by the vanity of being seen. I ought to except, indeed, those who turn devotees, and spend the greatest part of their time with the prieſt, either at church, or in their own houſes. Other amuſements they have none in this place, except private parties of card-playing, which are far from being expenſive. Nothing can be more parſimonious than the œconomy of theſe people: they live upon ſoupe and bouille, fiſh and ſallad: they never think of giving dinners, or entertaining their friends; they even ſave the expence of coffee and tea, tho' both are very cheap at Boulogne. They preſume that every perſon drinks coffee at home, immediately after dinner, which is always over by one o'clock; and in lieu of tea in the afternoon, they treat with a glaſs of ſherbet, or capillaire. In a word, I know not a more inſignificant ſet of mortals than the nobleſſe of Boulogne; helpleſs in themſelves, and uſeleſs to the community; without dignity, ſenſe, or ſentiment; contemptible from pride, and ridiculous from vanity. They pretend to be jealous of their rank, and will entertain no correspondence with the merchants, whom they term plebeian. They likewise keep at a great distance from strangers, on pretence of a delicacy in the article of punctilio: but, as I am informed, this stateliness is in a great measure affected, in order to conceal their poverty, which would appear to greater disadvantage if they admitted of a more familiar communication. Considering the vivacity of the French people, one would imagine they could not possibly lead such an insipid life, altogether unanimated by society or diversion. True it is, the only profane diversions of this place are a puppet-show and a mountebank; but then their religion affords a perpetual comedy. Their high masses, their feasts, their processions, their pilgrimages, confessions, images, tapers, robes, incense, benedictions, spectacles, representations, and innumerable ceremonies, which revolve almost incessantly, furnish a variety of entertainment from one end of the year to the other. If superstition implies *fear*, never was a word more misapplied than it is to the mummery of the religion of Rome. The people are so far from being impressed with awe and religious terror by this sort of machinery, that it amuses their imaginations in the most agreeable manner, and keeps them always in good humour. A Roman catholic longs as impatiently for the festival of *St Suaire*, or *St Croix*, or *St Veronique*, as a school-boy in

England for the reprefentation of punch and the devil; and there is generally as much laughing at one farce as at the other. Even when the defcent from the crofs is acted, in the holy week, with all the circumftances that ought naturally to infpire the graveft fentiments, if you caft your eyes among the multitude that croud the place, you will not difcover one melancholy face: all is prating, tittering, or laughing; and ten to one but you perceive a number of them employed in hiffing the female who perfonates the Virgin Mary. And here it may not be amifs to obferve, that the Roman catholics, not content with the infinite number of faints who really exifted, have not only perfonified *the crofs*, but made two female faints out of a piece of linen. *Veronique* or *Veronica*, is no other than a corruption of *vera icon*, or *vera effigies*, faid to be the exact reprefentation of our Saviour's face, impreffed upon a piece of linen, with which he wiped the fweat from his forehead in his way to the place of crucifixion. The fame is worfhipped under the name of *St Suaire*, from the Latin word *sudarium*. This fame handkerchief is faid to have had three folds, on every one of which was the impreffion; one of thefe remains at Jerufalem, a fecond was brought to Rome, and a third was conveyed to Spain. Baronius fays, there is a very ancient history of the *sancta facies* in the Vatican. Tillemont, however, looks upon the whole as a fable. Some suppose Veronica to be the same with St Hæmorrhoissa, the patroness of those who are afflicted with the piles, who make their joint invocations to her and St Fiacre, the son of a Scotch king, who lived and died a hermit in France. The troops of Henry V. of England are said to have pillaged the chapel of this Highland faint; who, in revenge, assisted his countrymen, in the French service, to defeat the English at Bauge, and afterwards afflicted Henry with the piles, of which he died. This prince complained, that he was not only plagued by the living Scots, but even persecuted by those who were dead.

I know not whether I may be allowed to compare the Romish religion to comedy, and Calvenism to tragedy. The first amuses the senses, and excites ideas of mirth and good humour; the other, like tragedy, deals in the passions of terror and pity. Step into a conventicle of dissenters, you will, ten to one, hear the minister holding forth upon the sufferings of Christ, or the torments of hell, and see many marks of religious horror in the faces of the hearers. This is perhaps one reason why the reformation did not succeed in France, among a volatile, giddy, unthinking people, shocked at the mortified appearances of the Calvinists; and accounts for its rapid progress among nations of a more melancholy turn of character and complexion; for, in the conversion of the multitude, reason is generally out of the question. Even the penance imposed upon the catholics is little more than mock mortification: a murderer is often acquitted with his confessor for saying three prayers extraordinary; and these easy terms, on which absolution is obtained, certainly encourage the repetition of the most enormous crimes. The pomp and ceremonies of this religion, together with the great number of holydays they observe, howsoever they may keep up the spirits of the commonalty, and help to diminish the sense of their own misery, must certainly, at the same time, produce a frivolous taste for frippery and shew, and encourage a habit of idleness, to which I, in a great measure, ascribe the extreme poverty of the lower people. Very near half of their time, which might be profitably employed in the exercise of industry, is lost to themselves and the community, in attendance upon the different exhibitions of religious mummery.

But as this letter has already run to an unconscionable length, I shall defer, till another occasion, what I have further to say on the people of this place, and in the mean time assure you, that I am always

Yours affectionately

LETTER V.

Boulogne September, 12, 1763.

DEAR SIR,

MY stay in this place now draws towards a period. 'Till within these few days I have continued bathing, with some advantage to my health, though the season has been cold and wet, and disagreeable. There was a fine prospect of a plentiful harvest in this neighbourhood. I used to have great pleasure in driving between the fields of wheat, oats, and barley; but the crop has been entirely ruined by the rain, and nothing is now to be seen on the ground but the tarnished straw, and the rotten spoils of the husbandman's labour. The ground scarce affords subsistence to a few flocks of meagre sheep, that crop the stubble, and the intervening grass; each flock under the protection of its shepherd, with his crook and dogs, who lyes every night in the midst of the fold, in a little thatched travelling lodge, mounted on a wheel-carriage. Here he passes the night, in order to defend his

LETTER V.

flock from the wolves, which are sometimes, especially in winter, very bold and desperate.

Two days ago we made an excursion with Mrs B—— and Capt. L—— to the village of Samers, on the Paris road, about three leagues from Boulogne. Here is a venerable abbey of Benedictines, well endowed, with large agreeable gardens prettily laid out. The monks are well lodged, and well entertained. Though restricted from flesh meals by the rules of their order, they are allowed to eat wild duck and teal, as a species of fish; and when they long for a good *bouillon*, or a partridge, or pullet, they have nothing to do but to say they are out of order. In that case the appetite of the patient is indulged in his own apartment. Their church is elegantly contrived, but kept in a very dirty condition. The greatest curiosity I saw in this place was an English boy, about eight or nine years old, from Dover, whom his father had sent hither to learn the French language. In less than eight weeks he was become captain of the boys of the place, spoke French perfectly well, and had almost forgot his mother tongue. But to return to the people of Boulogne.

The burghers here, as in other places, consist of merchants, shop-keepers, and artisans. Some of the merchants have got fortunes, by fitting out privateers during the war. A great many single ships were taken from the English, notwithstanding the good look-out of our cruisers, who were so alert, that the privateers from this coast were often taken in four hours after they sailed from the French harbour, and there is hardly a captain of an *armateur* in Boulogne, who has not been prisoner in England five or six times in the course of the war. They were fitted out at a very small expence, and used to run over in the night to the coast of England, where they hovered as English fishing smacks, until they kidnapped some coaster, with which they made the best of their way across the channel. If they fell in with a British cruizer, they surrendered without resistance: the captain was soon exchanged, and the loss of the proprietor was not great: if they brought their prize safe into harbour, the advantage was considerable. In time of peace the merchants of Boulogne deal in wine, brandies, and oil, imported from the South, and export fish, with the manufactures of France, to Portugal, and other countries; but the trade is not great. Here are two or three considerable houses of wine-merchants from Britain, who deal in Bourdeaux wine, with which they supply London and other parts of England, Scotland, and Ireland. The fishery of

LETTER V.

mackarel and herring is so considerable on this coast, that it is said to yield annually eight or nine hundred thousand livres, about thirty-five thousand pounds sterling.

The shop-keepers here drive a considerable traffic with the English smugglers, whose cutters are almost the only vessels one sees in the harbour of Boulogne, if we except about a dozen of those flat-bottomed boats, which raised such alarms in England in the course of the war. Indeed they seem to be good for nothing else, and perhaps they were built for this purpose only. The smugglers from the coast of Kent and Sussex pay English gold for great quantities of French brandy, tea, coffee and small wine, which they run from this country. They likewise by glass trinkets, toys, and coloured prints, which sell in England, for no other reason but that they come from France, as they may be had as cheap, and much better finished, of our own manufacture. They likewise take off ribbons, laces, linen and cambrics; though this branch of trade is chiefly in the hands of traders that come from London, and make their purchases at Dunkirk, where they pay no duties. It is certainly worth while for any traveller to lay in a stock of linen either at Dunkirk or Boulogne; the difference of the price at these two places is not great,

LETTER V.

Even here I have made a provision of shirts for one half of the money they would have cost in London. Undoubtedly the practice of smuggling is very detrimental to the fair trader, and carries considerable sums of money out of the kingdom, to enrich our rivals and enemies. The custom-house officers are very watchful, and make a great number of seizures nevertheless, the smugglers find their account in continuing this contraband commerce; and are said to indemnify themselves, if they save one cargo out of three. After all, the best way to prevent smuggling, is to lower the duties upon the commodities which are thus introduced. I have been told that the revenue upon tea has increased ever since the duty upon it was diminished. By the bye, the tea smuggled on the coast of Sussex is most execrable stuff. While I stayed at Hastings, for the conveniency of bathing, I must have changed my breakfast, if I had not luckily brought tea with me from London: yet we have as good tea at Boulogne for nine livres a pound, as that which sells at fourteen shillings at London.

The Bourgeois of this place seem to live at their ease, probably in consequence of their trade with the English. Their houses consist of the ground-floor, one storey above, and garrets. In those which are

LETTER V.

well furnished, you see pier-glasses and marble slabs; but the chairs are either paultry things, made with straw bottoms, which cost about a shilling a-piece, or old-fashioned, high-backed seats of needle-work, stuffed, very clumsy and incommodious. The tables are square fir-boards, that stand on edge in a corner, except when they are used, and then they are set upon cross legs that open and shut occasionally. The king of France dines off a board of this kind. Here is plenty of table-linen however. The poorest tradesman in Boulogne has a napkin on every corner, and silver forks with four prongs, which are used with the right hand, there being very little occasion for knives; for the meat is boiled, or roasted to rags. The French beds are so high, that sometimes one is obliged to mount them by the help of steps; and this is also the case in Flanders. They very seldom use feather-beds; but they ly upon a *paillasse*, or bag of straw, over which are laid two, and sometimes three mattrasses. Their testers are high and old-fashioned, and their curtains generally of thin bays, red or green, laced with tawdry yellow, in imitation of old. In some houses, however, one meets with furniture of stamped linen, but there is no such thing as a carpet to be seen, and the floors are in a very dirty condition.

They have not even the implements of cleanliness in this country. Every chamber is furnished with an *armoire*, or clothes-press, and a chest of drawers, of very clumsy workmanship. Every thing shews a deficiency in the mechanic arts. There is not a door nor a window that shuts close. The hinges, locks, and latches, are of iron, coarsely made, and ill contrived. The very chimnies are built so open, that they admit both rain and sun, and all of them smoke intolerably. If there is no cleanliness among these people, much less shall we find delicacy, which is the cleanliness of the mind. Indeed they are utter strangers to what we call common decency; and I could give you some high flavoured instances, at which even a native of Edinburgh would stop his nose. There are certain mortifying views of human nature, which undoubtedly ought to be concealed as much as possible, in order to prevent giving offence : and nothing can be more absurd, than to plead the difference of custom in different countries, in defence of those usages which cannot fail giving disgust to the organs and senses of all mankind. Will custom exempt from the imputation of gross indecency a French lady who shifts her frowsy smock in presence of a male visitant, and talks to him of her *lavement*, her *medicine*, and her *bidet* ! A

LETTER V.

Italian *signora* makes no scruple of telling you, she is such a day to begin a course of physic for the *pox*. The celebrated reformer of the Italian comedy introduces a child befouling itself on the stage, OE, NO TI SENTI? BISOGNA DESFASSARLO, (*fa cenno che sentesi mal odore.*) I have known a lady handed to the house of office by her admirer, who stood at the door, and entertained her with *bons mots* all the time she was within. But I should be glad to know whether it is possible for a fine lady to speak and act in this manner, without exciting ideas to her own disadvantage in the mind of every man who has any imagination left, and enjoys the entire use of his senses, howsoever she may be authorised by the customs of her country? There is nothing so vile or repugnant to nature, but you may plead prescription for it, in the customs of some nation or other. A Parisian likes mortified flesh a native of Legiboli will not taste his fish till it is quite putrefied: the civilized inhabitants of Kamschatka get drunk with the urine of their guests, whom they have already intoxicated: the Nova Zemblans make merry on train-oil: the Greenlanders eat in the same dish with their dogs: the Caffres, at the Cape of Good Hope, piss upon those whom they delight to honour, and feast upon a sheep's intestines with their contents, as the greatest dainty that can be presented. A true-bred Frenchman dips his fingers, imbrowned with snuff, into his plate filled with ragout: between every three mouthfuls, he produces his snuff box, and takes a fresh pinch, with the most graceful gesticulations; then he displays his handkerchief, which may be termed the *flag of abomination*, and, in the use of both, scatters his favours among those who have the happiness to sit near him. It must be owned, however, that a Frenchman will not drink out of a tankard in which, perhaps, a dozen of filthy mouths have flabbered, as is the custom in England. Here every individual has his own goblet, which stands before him, and he helps himself occasionally with wine, or water, or both, which likewise stand upon the table. But I know no custom more beastly than that of using water-glasses, in which polite company spirt, and squirt, and spue the filthy scourings of their gums, under the eyes of each other. I knew a lover cured of his passion, by seeing this nasty cascade discharged from the mouth of his mistress. I don't doubt but I shall live to see the day when the hospitable custom of the antient Egyptians will be revived; then a conveniency will be placed behind every chair in the company, with a proper provision of waste paper, that individuals may make themselves easy without parting company. I insist upon it, that this practice would not be more indelicate than that which is now in use. What then, you will say, must a man sit with his chops and fingers up to the ears and knuckles in grease? No; let those who cannot eat without defiling themselves, step into another room, provided with basons and towels. but I think it would be better to institute schools, where youth may learn to eat their victuals without daubing themselves, or giving offence to the eyes of one another.

The bourgeois of Boulogne have commonly soup and bouille at noon, and a roast, with a sallad, for supper; and at all their meals there is a desert of fruit. This indeed is the practice all over France. On meagre days they eat fish, omelettes, fried beans, fricassees of eggs and onions, and burnt cream. The tea which they drink in the afternoon is rather boiled than infused; it is sweetened all together with coarse sugar, and drank with an equal quantity of boiled milk.

We had the honour to be entertained the other day by our landlord, Mr B——, who spared no cost on this banquet, exhibited for the glory of France. He had invited a new-married couple, together with the husband's mother, and the lady's father, who was one of the noblesse of Montreul, his name Monf. L——y. There were likewise some merchants of the town, and Monf. B——'s uncle, a facetious little man, who had served in the English navy, and was as big and as round as a hogshead: we were likewise favoured with the company of father K——, a native of Ireland, who is *vicaire* or curate of the parish; and among the guests was Monf. L——y's son, a pretty boy, about thirteen or fourteen years of age. The *repas* served up in three services, or courses, with *entrees* and *hors d'œuvres*, exclusive of the fruit, consisted of above twenty dishes, extremely well dressed by the *rotisseur*, who is the best cook I ever knew, in France or elsewhere, but the *plats* were not presented with much order. Our young ladies did not seem to be much used to do the honours of the table. The most extraordinary circumstance that I observed on this occasion was, that all the French who were present ate of every dish that appeared; and I am told, that if there had been an hundred articles more, they would have had a trial of each. This is what they call doing justice to the founder. Monf. L——y was placed at the head of the table; and indeed he was the oracle and orator of the company; tall, thin, and weather-beaten, not unlike the picture of Don Quixote after he had lost his teeth. He had been *garre du corps*, or life-guardman at Versailles; and by virtue of this office he was perfectly well acquainted with the persons of the king and the dauphin, with the characters of the ministers and grandees, and, in a word, with all the secrets of state, on which he held forth with equal solemnity and elocution. He exclaimed against the Jesuits, and the farmers of the revenue, who, he said, had ruined France. Then addressing himself to me, asked, if the English did not every day drink to the health of *madame la marquise?* I did not at first comprehend his meaning; but answered in general, that the English were not deficient in complaisance for the ladies. "Ah! (cried he) she is the best "friend they have in the world. If it "had not been for her, they would not "have such reason to boast of the advan- "tages of the war." I told him the only conquest which the French had made was atchieved by one of her generals. I meant the taking of Mahon. But I did not chuse to prosecute the discourse, remembring that, in the year 1749, I had like to have had an affair with a Frenchman at Ghent, who affirmed, that all the battles gained by the great Duke of Marlborough were purposely lost by the French generals, in order to bring the schemes of madame de Maintenon into difgrace. This is no bad refource for the national vanity of thefe people: though, in general, they are really perfuaded that theirs is the richeft, the braveft, the happieft, and the moft powerful nation under the fun; and therefore, without fome fuch caufe, they muft be invincible. By the bye, the common people here ftill frighten their wayward children with the name of *Marlborough*. Mr B——'s fon, who was nurfed at a peafant's houfe, happening one day, after he was brought home, to be in difgrace with his father, who threatned to correct him, the child ran for protection to his mother, crying. " *Faites* " *fortir ce vilain Malbroug.*" It is amazing to hear a fenfible Frenchman affert, that the revenues of France amount to four hundred millions of livres, about twenty millions fterling, clear of all incumbrances, when in fact their clear revenue is not much above ten. Without all doubt they have reafon to inveigh againft the *fermiers generaux*, who opprefs the people in raifing the taxes, not above two thirds of which are brought into the kings coffers: the reft enriches themfelves, and enables them to bribe high for the protection of the great, which is the only fupport they have againft the remonftrances of the ftates and parliaments, and the suggestions of common sense; which will ever demonstrate this to be, of all others, the most pernicious method of supplying the necessities of government.

Monsf. L——y seasoned the severity of his political apothegms with intermediate sallies of mirth and gallantry. He ogled the venerable gentlewoman his *commere*, who sat by him. He looked, sighed and languished, sung tender songs, and kissed the old lady's hand with all the ardour of a youthful admirer. I unfortunately congratulated him on having such a pretty young gentleman to his son. He answered, sighing, that the boy had talents, but did not put them to a proper use—" long before I attained his age (said he) I had finished my rhetoric." Captain B——, who had eaten himself black in the face, and, with the napkin under his chin, was no bad representation of Sancho Panza in the suds, with the dishclout about his neck, when the Duke's scullions insisted upon having him; this sea wit, turning to the boy, with a waggish leer, " I suppose (said he) you don't understand the figure of *amplification* so well as Monsieur your father." At that instant, one of the nieces, who knew her uncle to be very ticklish, touched him under the short ribs, on which the little man attempted to spring up, but lost the centre of gravity. He overturned his own plate in the lap of the person that sat next to him, and falling obliquely upon his own chair, both tumbled down upon the floor together, to the great discomposure of the whole company; for the poor man would have been actually strangled, had not his nephew loosed his stock with great expedition. Matters being once more adjusted, and the captain condoled on his disaster, Monf. L——y took it in his head to read his son a lecture upon filial obedience. This was mingled with some sharp reproof, which the boy took so ill, that he retired. The old lady observed that he had been too severe. her daughter-in-law, who was very pretty, said her brother had given him too much reason; hinting, at the same time, that he was addicted to some terrible vices; upon which several individuals repeated the interjection, ah! ah! "Yes (said Monf. L——y, with a rueful aspect) the boy has a pernicious turn for gaming; in one afternoon he lost, at billiards, such a sum as gives me horror to think of it." "Fifty sols in one afternoon," (cried the sister.) "Fifty sols! exclaimed the mother-in-law, with marks of astonishment, that's too much—that's too much!—he's to blame—he's to blame! but youth, you know Monf. L——y —ah! vive la jeunesse!" " et l'amour!" cried the father wiping his eyes, squeezing her hand, and looking tenderly upon her. Mr B—— took this opportunity to bring in the young gentleman, who was admitted into favour, and received a second exhortation. Thus harmony was restored, and the entertainment concluded with fruit, coffee, and *liqueurs*.

When a bourgeois of Boulogne takes the air, he goes in a one horse-chaise, which is here called *cabriolet*, and hires it for half-a-crown a day. There are also travelling chaises, which hold four persons, two seated with their faces to the horses, and two behind their backs; but those vehicles are all very ill made, and extremely inconvenient. The way of riding most used in this place is on ass-back. You will see every day, in the skirts of the town, a great number of females thus mounted, with the feet on either side occasionally, according as the wind blows, so that sometimes the right and sometimes the left hand guides the beast: but in other parts of France, as well as in Italy, the ladies sit on horseback with their legs astride, and are provided with drawers for that purpose.

When I said the French people were kept in good humour by the fopperies of their religion, I did not mean that there were no gloomy spirits among them: there will be fanatics in religion, while there are people of a saturnine disposition, and melancholy turn of mind. The character of a *devotee*, which is hardly known in England, is very common here. You see them walking to and from church at all hours, in their hoods and long camblet cloaks, with a slow pace, demure aspect, and downcast eye. Those who are poor become very troublesome to the monks, with their scruples and cases of conscience: you may see them on their knees, at the confessional, every hour in the day. The rich *devotee* has her favourite confessor, whom she consults and regales in private, at her own house; and this spiritual director generally governs the whole family. For my part, I never knew a fanatic that was not an hypocrite at bottom. Their pretensions to superior sanctity, and an absolute conquest over all the passions, which human reason was never yet able to subdue, introduce a habit of dissimulation, which, like all other habits, is confirmed by use, till at length they become adepts in the art and science of hypocrisy. Enthusiasm and hypocrisy are by no means incompatible. The wildest fanatics I ever knew, were real sensualists in their way of living, and cunning cheats in their dealings with mankind.

Among the lower class of people at Boulogne, those who take the lead are the sea-faring men, who live in one quarter, divided into classes, and registered for the service of the king. They are hardy and raw boned, exercise the trade of fishermen and boatmen, and propagate like rabbits. They have put themselves under the protection of a miraculous image of the Virgin Mary, which is kept in one of their churches, and every year carried in procession. According to the legend, this image was carried off, with other pillage, by the English, when they took Boulogne, in the reign of Henry VIII. The lady, rather than reside in England, where she found a great many heretics, trusted herself alone, in an open boat, and crossed the sea to the road of Boulogne, where she was seen waiting for a pilot. Accordingly a boat put off to her assistance, and brought her safe into the harbour: since which time she has continued to patronize the watermen of Boulogne. At present she is very black and very ugly, besides being cruelly mutilated in different parts of her body, which I suppose have been imputated, and converted into tobacco-stoppers; but once a-year she is dressed in very rich attire, and carried in procession, with a silver boat, provided at the expence of the sailors. That vanity which characterises the French extends even to the canaille: the lowest creature among them is sure to have her ear-rings and golden cross hanging about her neck. Indeed this last is an implement of superstition as well as of dress, without which no female appears. The common people here, as in all countries where they live poorly and dirtily, are hard-featured, and of very brown, or rather tawny complexions. As they seldom eat meat, their juices are destitute of that animal oil which gives a plumpness and smoothness to the skin, and defends those fine capillaries from the injuries of the weather, which would otherwise coalesce, or be shrunk up, so as to impede the circulation on the external surface of the body. As for the dirt, it undoubtedly blocks up the pores of the skin, and disorders the perspiration; consequently must contribute to the scurvy itch, and other cutaneous distempers.

In the quarter of the *matelots* at Boulogne, there is a number of poor Canadians, who were removed from the island of St Jon, in the gulph of St Laurence, when it was reduced by the English. These people are maintained at the expence of the king, who allows them soldier's pay, that is five sols, or twopence halfpenny a day, or rather three sols and ammunition bread. How the soldiers contrive to subsist upon this wretched allowance, I cannot compre-

LETTER V.

friend; but it must be owned, that those invalids who do duty at Boulogne betray no marks of want. They are hale and stout, neatly and decently cloathed, and, on the whole, look better than the pensioners of Chelsea.

About three weeks ago I was favoured with a visit by one Mr M——, an English gentleman, who seems far gone in a consumption. He passed the last winter at Nismes in Languedoc, and found himself much better in the beginning of summer, when he embarked at Cette, and returned by sea to England. He soon relapsed, however, and (as he imagines) in consequence of a cold caught at sea. He told me his intention was to try the South again and even to go as far as Italy. I advised him to make trial of the air of Nice, where I myself proposed to reside. He seemed to relish my advice, and proceeded towards Paris in his own carriage.

I shall to-morrow ship my great chests on board of a ship bound to Bourdeaux; they are directed, and recommended to the care of a merchant of that place, who will forward them by Thoulouse, and the canal of Languedoc, to his correspondent at Cette, which is the sea-port of Montpelier. The charge of their conveyance to Bourdeaux does not exceed one guinea: they consist of two very large chests and a trunk, about a thousand pounds weight and the expence of transporting them from Bourdeaux to Cette, will not exceed thirty livres: they are already sealed with lead at the custom-house, that they may be exempted from further visitation: this is a precaution which every traveller takes both by sea and land: he must likewise provide himself with a *passe avant* at the bureau, otherwise he may be stopped and rummaged at every town through which he passes. I have hired a berlin and four horses to Paris, for fourteen lou'dors, two of which the *voiturier* is obliged to pay for a permission from the farmers of the poste; for every thing is farmed in this country; and if you hire a carriage, as I have done, you must pay twelve livres, or half a guinea, for every person that travels in it. The common coach between Calais and Paris is such a vehicle as no man would use, who has any regard to his own ease and convenience; and it travels at the pace of an English waggon.

In ten days I shall set out on my journey: and I shall leave Boulogne with regret. I have been happy in the acquaintance of Mrs B———, and a few British families in the place; and it was my good fortune to meet here with two honest gentlemen whom I had formerly known at Paris, as well as with some of my countrymen, officers in the service of France. My next will be from Paris. Remember me to our friends at A———'s. I am a little heavy-hearted at the prospect of removing to such a distance from you. It is a moot point whether I shall ever return. My health is very precarious. Adieu.

LETTER VI.

Paris, October 12, 1 6

DEAR SIR,

OF our journey from Boulogne I have little to say. The weather was favourable, and the roads were in tollerable order. We found good accommodation at Montreuil and Amiens, but in every other place where we stopped, we met with abundance of dirt, and the most flagrant imposition. I shall not pretend to describe the cities of Abeville and Amiens, which we saw only *en passant*; nor take up your time with an account of the stables and palace of Chantilly, belonging to the Prince of Conde, which we visited the last day of our journey; nor shall I detain you with a detail of the *Tresors de St Denis*, which, together with the tombs in the abbey church, afforded us some amusement while our dinner was getting ready. All these particulars are mentioned in twenty different books of tours, travels, and directions, which you have often perused. I shall only observe, that the abbey church is the lightest piece of Gothic architecture I have seen, and the air within seems perfectly free from that damp and moisture, so perceivable in all our old cathedrals. This must be owing to the nature of its situation. There are some fine marble statues that adorn the tombs of certain individuals here interred; but they are mostly in the French-taste, which is quite contrary to the simplicity of the ancients. Their attitudes are affected, unnatural, and desultory; and their draperies fantastic; or, as one of our English artists expressed himself, *they are all of a flutter*. As for the treasures which are shewn on certain days to the populace gratis, they are contained in a number of presses or armoires; and, if the stones are genuine, they must be inestimable; but this I cannot believe. Indeed I have been told, that what they shew as diamonds are no more than composition; nevertheless, exclusive of these, there are some rough stones of great value, and many curiosities worth seeing. The monk that shewed them was the very image of our friend Hamilton, both in his looks and manner.

LETTER VI.

I have one thing very extraordinary to observe of the French auberges, which seems to be a remarkable deviation from the general character of the nation. The landlords, hostesses, and servants of the inns upon the road, have not the least dash of complaisance in their behaviour to strangers. Instead of coming to the door to receive you as in England, they take no manner of notice of you; but leave you to find or inquire your way into the kitchen, and there you must ask several times for a chamber, before they seem willing to conduct you up stairs. In general, you are served with the appearance of the most mortifying indifference, at the very time they are laying schemes for fleecing you of your money. It is a very odd contrast between France and England: in the former all the people are complaisant but the publicans; in the latter there is hardly any complaisance but among the publicans. When I said all the people in France, I ought also to except those vermin who examine the baggage of travellers in different parts of the kingdom. Although our portmanteaus were sealed with lead, and we were provided with a passe-avant from the douane, our coach was searched at the gate of Paris by which we entered; and the women were obliged to get out, and stand in the open street, till this operation was performed.

LETTER VI.

I had desired a friend to provide lodgings for me at Paris, in the Fauxbourg St Germain; and accordingly we found ourselves accommodated at the hotel de Montmorency, with a first floor, which costs me ten livres a day. I should have put up with it had it been less polite; but as I have only a few days to stay in this place, and some visits to receive, I am not sorry that my friend has exceeded his commission. I have been guilty of another piece of extravagance in hiring a *caroffe de remife*, for which I pay twelve livres a day. Besides the article of visiting, I could not leave Paris without carrying my wife and the girls to see the most remarkable places in and about this capital, such as the Luxemburg, the Palais-royal, the Thuilleries, the Louvre, the Invalids, the Gobelins, &c. together with Versailles, Trianon, Marli, Meudon, and Choisii; and therefore I thought the difference in point of expence would not be great, between a caroffe de remife and a hackney coach. The first are extremely elegant, if not too much ornamented; the last are very shabby and disagreeable. Nothing gives me such chagrin as the necessity I am under to hire a *valet de place*, as my own servant does not speak the language. You cannot conceive with what eagerness and dexterity those rascally valets exert themselves in pillaging strangers. There

LETTER VI.

always one ready in waiting on your arrival, who begins by assisting your own servant to unload your baggage, and interests himself in your affairs with such artful officiousness, that you will find it difficult to shake him off, even though you are determined beforehand against hiring any such domestic. He produces recommendations from his former masters, and the people of the house vouch for his honesty. The truth is, those fellows are very handy, useful, and obliging; and so far honest, that they will not steal in the usual way. You may safely trust one of them to bring you a hundred loui dores from your banker; but they fleece you without mercy in every other article of expence. They lay all your tradesmen under contribution; your taylor, barbar, mantua maker, milliner, perfumer, shoemaker, mercer, jeweller, hatter, traiteur, and wine-merchant. even the bourgeois who owns your coach pays him twenty sols *per* day. His wages amount to twice as much; so that I imagine the fellow that serves me makes above ten shillings a day, besides his victuals, which, by the bye, he has no right to demand. Living at Paris, to the best of my recollection, is very near twice as dear as it was fifteen years ago; and, indeed this is the case in London; a circumstance that must be undoubtedly owing to an increase of.

taxes; for I don't find that in the articles of eating and drinking the French people are more luxurious than they were heretofore. I am told the *entrees*, or duties, paid upon provision imported into Paris, are very heavy. All manner of butchers meat and poultry are extremely good in this place. The beef is excellent. The wine which is generally drank is a very thin kind of Burgundy. I can by no means relish their cookery; but one breakfasts deliciously upon their *petit pains* and their *pates* of butter, which last is exquisite.

The common people, and even the bourgeois of Paris, live, at this season, chiefly on bread and grapes, which is undoubtedly very wholsome fare. If the same simplicity of diet prevailed in England, we should certainly undersell the French at all foreign markets for they are very slothful with all their vivacity; and the great number of their holidays not only encourages this lazy disposition, but actually robs them of one half of what their labour would otherwise produce; so that, if our common people were not so expensive in their living, that is, in their eating and drinking, labour might be afforded cheaper in England than in France. There are three young lusty hussies, nieces or daughters of a blacksmith that lives just opposite to my windows, who do nothing from morning till night. They eat grapes and bread from seven till nine, from nine till twelve they dress their hair, and are all the afternoon gaping at the window to view passengers. I don't perceive that they give themselves the trouble either to make their beds, or clean their apartment. The same spirit of idleness and dissipation I have observed in every part of France, and among every class of people.

Every object seems to have shrunk in its dimensions since I was last in Paris. The Louvre, the Palais-royal, the bridges, and the river Seine, by no means answer the ideas I had formed of them from my former observation. When the memory is not very correct, the imagination always betrays her into such extravagances. When I first revisited my own country, after an absence of fourteen years, I found every thing diminished in the same manner, and I could scarce believe my own eyes.

Notwithstanding the gay disposition of the French, their houses are all gloomy. In spite of all the ornaments that have been lavished on Versailles, it is a dismal habitation. The apartments are dark, ill furnished, dirty, and unprincely. Take the castle, chapel, and garden all together, they make a most fantastic composition of magnificence and littleness, taste and foppery. After all, it is in England only where we muſt look for cheerful apartments, gay furniture, neatneſs and convenience. There is a ſtrange incongruity in the French genius. With all their volatility, prattle, and fondneſs for *bons mots*, they delight in a ſpecies of drawling, melancholy church-muſic. Their moſt favourite dramatic pieces are almoſt without incident; and the dialogue of their comedies conſiſts of moral, inſipid apophthegms, entirely deſtitute of wit or repartee. I know what I hazard by this opinion among the implicit admirers of Lully, Racine and Moliere.

I don't talk of the buſts, the ſtatues and pictures which abound at Verſailles, and other places in and about Paris, particularly the great collection of capital pieces in the Palais-royal belonging to the Duke of Orleans. I have neither capacity nor inclination to give a critique on theſe *chef d' œuvres*, which indeed would take up a whole volume. I have ſeen this great magazine of painting three times with aſtoniſhment; but I ſhould have been better pleaſed if there had not been half the number one is bewildered in ſuch a profuſion, as not to know where to begin, and hurried away before there is time to conſider one piece with any ſort of deliberation. Beſides, the rooms are all dark, and a great many of the pictures hang in a bad light. As for Trianon, Marli, and Choiſſi, they are no more than pidgeon-houses, in respect to palaces; and, notwithstanding the extravagant eulogiums which you have heard of the French king's houses, I will venture to affirm that the king of England is better, I mean more comfortably lodged. I ought, however, to except Fontainbleau, which I have not seen.

The city of Paris is said to be five leagues or fifteen miles in circumference; and if it is really so, it must be much more populous than London; for the streets are very narrow, and the houses very high, with a different family on every floor. But I have measured the best plans of these two royal cities, and am certain that Paris does not take up near so much ground as London and Westminster occupy; and I suspect the number of its inhabitants is also exaggerated by those who say it amounts to eight hundred thousand, that is two hundred thousand more than are contained in the bills of mortality. The hotels of the French noblesse, at Paris, take up a great deal of room, with their court-yards and gardens; and so do their convents and churches. It must be owned, indeed, that their streets are wonderfully crowded with people and carriages.

The French begin to imitate the English, but only in such particulars as render them worthy of imitation. When I was last at

Paris, no person of any condition, male or female, appeared, but in full dress, even when obliged to come out early in the morning, and there was not such a thing to be seen as a *peruke ronde*, but at present I see a number of frocks and scratches in a morning, in the streets of this metropolis. They have set up a *petite poste*, on the plan of our penny-post, with some improvements; and I am told there is a scheme on foot for supplying every house with water, by leaden pipes, from the river Seine. They have even adopted our practice of the cold bath, which is taken very conveniently, in wooden houses, erected on the side of the river, the water of which is let in and out occasionally, by cocks fixed in the sides of the bath. There are different rooms for the different sexes: the accommodations are good, and the expence is a trifle. The tapestry of the Gobelins is brought to an amazing degree of perfection; and I am surprised that this furniture is not more in fashion among the great, who alone are able to purchase it. It would be a most elegant and magnificent ornament, which would always nobly distinguish their apartments from those of an inferior rank; and in this they would run no risque of being rivalled by the bourgeois. At the village of Chaillot, in the neighbourhood of Paris, they make beauiful carpets and screen-work; and this is the more extraordinary, as there are hardly any carpets used in this kingdom. In almost all the lodging-houses, the floors are of brick, and have no other kind of cleaning than that of being sprinkled with water, and swept once a day. These brick floors, the stone stairs, the want of wainscotting in the rooms, and the thick party walls of stone, are however good preservatives against fire, which seldom does any damage in this city. Instead of wainscotting, the walls are covered with tapestry or damask. The beds in general are very good, and well ornamented with testers and curtains.

Fifteen years ago the river Seine, within a mile of Paris, was as solitary as if it had run through a desart. At present the banks of it are adorned with a number of elegant houses and plantations, as far as Marli. I need not mention the machine at this place for raising water, because I know you are well acquainted with its construction; nor shall I say any thing more of the city of Paris, but that there is a new square, built upon an elegant plan, at the end of the garden of the Thuilleries: it is called *Place de Louis* XV. and, in the middle of it, there is a good equestrian statue of the reigning king.

You have often heard that Louis XIV.

frequently regretted that his country did not afford gravel for the walks of his gardens, which are covered with a white loose sand, very disagreeable both to the eyes and feet of those who walk upon it; but this is a vulgar mistake. There is plenty of gravel on the road between Paris and Versailles, as well as in many other parts of this kingdom; but the French, who are all for glare and glitter, think the other is more gay and agreeable. one would imagine they did not feel the burning reflection from the white sand, which in summer is almost intolerable.

In the character of the French, considered as a people, there are undoubtedly many circumstances truly ridiculous. You know the fashionable people, who go a hunting, are equipped with their jack-boots, bag wigs, swords and pistols: but I saw the other day a scene still more grotesque. On the road to Choissi, a *fiacre*, or hackney-coach, stopped, and out came five or six men, armed with musquets, who took post each behind a separate tree. I asked our servant who they were, imagining they might be *archers*, or footpads of justice, in pursuit of some malefactor. But guess my surprise, when the fellow told me they were gentlemen *a la chasse*. They were in fact come out from Paris, in this equipage, to take the diversion of hare-hunting; that is, of shooting from behind a tree at the hares that chanced to pass. Indeed, if they had nothing more in view but to destroy the game, this was a very effectual method; for the hares are in such plenty in this neighbourhood, that I have seen a dozen together, in the same field. I think this way of hunting, in a coach or chariot, might be properly adopted at London, in favour of those aldermen of the city who are too unweildy to follow the hounds on horseback.

The French, however, with all their absurdities, preserve a certain ascendency over us, which is very disgraceful to our nation; and this appears in nothing more than in the article of dress. We are contented to be thought their apes in fashion: but, in fact, we are slaves to their tailors, mantua-makers, barbers, and other tradesmen. One would be apt to imagine that our own tradesmen had joined them in a combination against us. When the natives of France come to London, they appear in all public places with clothes made according to the fashion of their own country, and this fashion is generally admired by the English: why, therefore, don't we follow it implicitly? No; we pique ourselves upon a most ridiculous deviation from the very modes we admire, and please ourselves with thinking this deviation is a mark of our spirit and liberty: but we have not spirit enough to persist in this deviation when we visit their country; otherwise, perhaps, they would come to admire and follow our example: for certainly, in point of true taste, the fashions of both countries are equally absurd. At present the skirts of the English descend from the fifth rib to the calf of the leg, and give the coat the form of a Jewish gaberdine; and our hats seem to be modelled after that which Pistol wears upon the stage. In France, the haunch buttons and pocket-holes are within half a foot of the coat's extremity; their hats look as if they had been pared round the brims, and the crown is covered with a kind of cordage, which, in my opinion, produces a very beggarly effect. In every other circumstance of dress, male and female, the contrast between the two nations appears equally glaring. What is the consequence? when an Englishman comes to Paris, he cannot appear until he has undergone a total metamorphosis. At his first arrival he finds it necessary to send for the taylor, peruquier, hatter, shoemaker, and every other tradesman concerned in the equipment of the human body. He must even change his buckles, and the form of his ruffles; and, though at the risque of his life, suit his clothes to the mode of the season. For example, though the wea ther should be never so cold, he must wear his *habit d' ete*, or *de mi-saison*, without presuming to put on a warm dress before the day which fashion has fixed for that purpose; and neither old age nor infirmity will excuse a man for wearing his hat upon his head, either at home or abroad. Females are (if possible) still more subject to the caprices of fashion; and as the articles of their dress are more manifold, it is enough to make a man's heart ake to see his wife surrounded by a multitude of *cotturieres*, milliners, and tire-women. All her sacks and negligees must be altered and new trimmed. She must have new caps, new laces, new shoes, and her hair new cut. She must have her taffaties for the summer, her flowered silks for the spring and autumn, her sattins and damasks for winter. The good man, who used to wear the *beau drap d' Angleterre*, quite plain all the year round, with a long bob, or tye perriwig, must here provide himself with a camblet suit trimmed with silver for spring and autumn, with silk cloaths for summer, and cloth laced with gold, or velvet for winter; and he must wear his bag-wig *a la pigeon*. This variety of dress is absolutely indispensible for all those who pretend to any rank above the mere bourgeois. On his return to his own country all this frippery is useless. He cannot appear in

London until he has undergone another thorough metamorphosis; so that he will have some reason to think, that the tradesmen of Paris and London have combined to lay him under contribution: and they, no doubt, are the directors who regulate the fashions in both capitals; the English, however, in a subordinate capacity. for the puppets of their making will not pass at Paris, nor indeed in any other part of Europe; whereas a French petite-maitre is reckoned a complete figure every where, London not excepted. Since it is so much the humour of the English at present to run abroad, I wish they had antigallican spirit enough to produce themselves in their own genuine English dress, and treat the French modes with the same philosophical contempt which was shewn by an honest gentleman distinguished by the name of Wig-Middleton. That unshaken patriot still appears in the same kind of scratch perriwig, skimming-dish hat, and slit sleeve, which were worn five-and-twenty years ago, and has invariably persisted in this garb, in defiance of all the revolutions of the mode. I remember a student in the Temple, who, after a long and learned investigation of the το καλον, or *beautiful*, had resolution enough to let his beard grow, and wore it in all public places, untill his heir at law applied for a commission of lunacy against him; then he submitted to the razor, rather than run any risque of being found *non compos*.

Before I conclude, I must tell you, that the most reputable shop-keepers and tradesmen of Paris think it no disgrace to practise the most shameful imposition. I myself know an instance of one of the most creditable *marchands* in this capital, who demanded six francs an ell for some luteting, laying his hand upon his breast at the same time, and declaring *en conscience*, that it had cost him within three sols of the money: yet, in less than three minutes, he sold it for four and a half; and when the buyer upbraided him with his former declaration, he shrugged up his shoulders, saying, *Il faut marchander*. I don't mention this as a particular instance. The same mean disingenuity is universal all over France, as I have been informed by several persons of veracity.

The next letter you have from me will probably be dated at Nismes, or Montpelier. Mean-while, I am ever

Yours.

LETTER VII.

To Mrs M——

Paris, October, 12, 1763

MADAM,

I Shall be much pleased if the remarks I have made on the characters of the French people can afford you the satisfaction you require. With respect to the ladies, I can only judge from their exteriors; but, indeed, these are so characteristic, that one can hardly judge amiss; unless we suppose that a woman of taste and sentiment may be so over ruled by the absurdity of what is called fashion, as to reject reason, and disguise nature, in order to become ridiculous or frightful. That this may be the case with some individuals is very possible. I have known it happen in our own country, where the follies of the French are adopted, and exhibited in the most aukward imitation: but the general prevalence of those preposterous modes is a plain proof that there is a general want of taste, and a general depravity of nature. I shall not pretend to describe the particulars of a French lady's dress; these you are much better acquainted with than I can pretend to be: but this I will be bold to affirm, that France is the general reservoir from which all the abſurdities of falſe taſte, luxury and extravagance have overflowed the different kingdoms and ſtates of Europe. The ſprings that fill this reservoir, are no other than vanity and ignorance. It would be ſuperfluous to attempt proving from the nature of things, from the firſt principles and uſe of dreſs, as well as from the conſideration of natural beauty, and the practice of the Ancients, who certainly underſtood it as well as the connoiſſeurs of theſe days, that nothing can be more monſtrous, inconvenient, and contemptible, than the faſhion of modern drapery. You yourſelf are well aware of all its defects, and have often ridiculed them in my hearing. I ſhall only mention one particular of dreſs eſſential to the faſhion in this country, which ſeems to me to carry human affectation to the very fartheſt verge of folly and extravagance; that is, the manner in which the faces of the ladies are primed and painted. When the Indian chiefs were in England, every body ridiculed their prepoſterous method of painting their cheeks and eye-lids; but this ridicule was wrong placed. Thoſe critics ought to have conſidered, that the Indians do not uſe paint to make themſelves agreeable; but in order to be the more terrible to their enemies. It is generally fuppofed, I think, that your fex make ufe of *fard* and vermilion for very different purpofes, namely, to help a bad or faded complection, to heighten the graces, or conceal the defects of nature, as well as the ravages of time. I fhall not enquire at prefent, whether it is juft and honeft to impofe in this manner, on mankind: if it is not honeft, it may be allowed to be artful and politic, and fhews, at leaft, a defire of being agreeable. But to lay it on as the fafhion in France prefcribes to all the ladies of condition, who indeed cannot appear without this badge of diftinction, is to difguife themfelves in fuch a manner as to render them odious and deteftable to every fpectator who has the leaft relifh left for nature and propriety. As for the *fard*, or *white*, with which their necks and fhoulders are plaiftered, it may be in fome meafure excufable, as their fkins are naturally brown or fallow; but the *rouge*, which is daubed on their faces, from the chin up to the eyes, without the leaft art or dexterity, not only deftroys all diftinction of features, but renders the afpect really frightful, or at beft conveys nothing but ideas of difguft and averfion. You know, that without this horrible mafque no married lady is admitted at court, or in any polite affembly; and that it is a mark of diſtinction which no bourgeoiſe dare aſſume. Ladies of faſhion only have the privilege of expoſing themſelves in theſe ungracious colours. As their faces are concealed under a falſe complection, ſo their heads are covered with a vaſt load of falſe hair, which is frizzled on the forehead ſo as exactly to reſemble the woolly heads of the Guinea Negroes. As to the natural hue of it, this is a matter of no conſequence, for powder makes every head of hair of the ſame colour; and no woman appears in this country, from the moment ſhe riſes till night, without being compleately whitened. Powder or meal was firſt uſed in Europe by the Poles, to conceal their ſcald heads; but the preſent faſhion of uſing it, as well as the modiſh method of dreſſing the hair, muſt have been borrowed from the Hottentots, who greaſe their woolly heads with mutton-ſuet, and then paſte it over with the powder called *buchu*. In like manner, the hair of our fine ladies is frizzled into the appearance of negroes wool, and ſtiffened with an abominable paſte of hog's greaſe, tallow, and white powder. The preſent faſhion, therefore, of painting the face, and adorning the head, adopted by the beau-monde in France, is taken from thoſe two polite nations the Chickeſaws of America and the Hottentots of Afric. On the whole, when

I see one of those fine creatures sailing along, in her taudry robes of silk and gauze, frilled, and flounced, and furbelowed, with her false locks, her false jewels, her paint, her patches and perfumes, I cannot help looking upon her as the vilest piece of sophistication that art ever produced.

This hideous masque of painting, though destructive of all beauty, is however favourable to natural homeliness and deformity. It accustoms the eyes of the other sex, and in time reconciles them to frightful objects; it disables them from perceiving any distinction of features between woman and woman, and, by reducing all faces to a level, gives every female an equal chance for an admirer; being in this particular analagous to the practice of the ancient Lacedemonians, who were obliged to chuse their help-mates in the dark. In what manner the insides of their heads are furnished, I would not presume to judge from the conversation of a very few to whom I have had access: but from the nature of their education, which I have heard described, and the natural vivacity of their tempers, I should expect neither sense, sentiment, nor discretion. From the nursery they are allowed, and even encouraged, to say every thing that comes uppermost; by which means they acquire a volubility of tongue, and a set of phrases,

LETTER VII.

which constitutes what is called polite conversation. At the same time they obtain an absolute conquest over all sense of shame, or rather, they avoid acquiring this troublesome sensation; for it is certainly no innate idea. Those who have not governesses at home, are sent, for a few years, to a convent, where they lay in a fund of superstition that serves them for life: but I never heard they had the least opportunity of cultivating the mind, of exercising the powers of reason, or of imbibing a taste for letters, or any rational or useful accomplishment. After being taught to prattle, to dance and play at cards, they are deemed sufficiently qualified to appear in the *grande monde*, and to perform all the duties of that high rank and station in life. In mentioning cards, I ought to observe, that they learn to play not barely for amusement, but also with a view to advantage; and, indeed, you seldom meet with a native of France, whether male or female, who is not a complete gamester, well versed in all the subtleties and finesses of the art. This is likewise the case all over Italy. A lady of great house in Piedmont, having four sons, makes no scruple to declare, that the first shall represent the family, the second enter into the army, the third into the church, and that she will breed the fourth a gamester. These noble adventurers devote themselves in a particular manner to the entertainment of travellers from our country, because the English are supposed to be full of money, rash, incautious, and utterly ignorant of play. But such a sharper is most dangerous, when he hunts in couple with a female. I have known a French count and his wife, who found means to lay the most wary under contribution. He was smooth, supple, officious, and attentive: she was young, handsome, unprincipled, and artful. If the Englishman marked for prey was found upon his guard against the designs of the husband, the madam plied him on the side of gallantry. She displayed all the attractions of her person. She sung, danced, ogled, sighed, complimented, and complained. If he was insensible to all her charms, she flattered his vanity, and piqued his pride, by extolling the wealth and generosity of the English; and if he proved deaf to all these insinuations, she as her last stake, endeavoured to interest his humanity and compassion. She expatiated, with tears in her eyes, on the cruelty and indifference of her great relations; represented that her husband was no more than the cadet of a noble family; that his provision was by no means suitable either to the dignity of his rank, or the generosity of his disposition: that he had

LETTER VII.

a law suit of great consequence depending, which had drained all his finances; and, finally, that they should be both ruined, if they could not find some generous friend who would accommodate them with a sum of money to bring the cause to a determination. Those who are not actuated by such scandalous motives, become gamesters from mere habit; and, having nothing more solid to engage their thoughts, or employ their time, consume the best part of their lives in this worst of all dissipation. I am not ignorant that there are exceptions from this general rule · I know that France has produced a Maintenon, a Sevigne, a Scuderi, a Dacier, and a Chatelet: but I would no more deduce the general character of the French ladies from these examples, than I would call a field of hemp a flower-garden, because there might be in it a few lilies or *renunculas* planted by the hand of accident.

Woman has been defined a weaker man. but in this country the men are, in my opinion more ridiculous and insignificant than the women They certainly are more disagreeable to a rational inquirer, because they are more troublesome. Of all the coxcombs on the face of the earth, a French *petit maitre* is the most impertinent: and they are all *petit maitres*, from the marquis who glitters in lace and embroidery, to the *garcon barbier* covered with meal, who struts with his hair in a long queue, and his hat under his arm. I have already observed, that vanity is the great and universal mover among all ranks and degrees of people in this nation; and as they take no pains to conceal or controul it, they are hurried by it into the most ridiculous, and indeed intollerable extravagance.

When I talk of the French nation, I must again except a great number of individuals from the general censure. Though I have a hearty contempt for the ignorance, folly, and presumption which characterise the generality, I cannot but respect the talents of many great men, who have eminently distinguished themselves in every art and science: these I shall always revere and esteem, as creatures of a superior species, produced, for the wise purposes of Providence, among the refuse of mankind. It would be absurd to conclude that the Welch or Highlanders are a gigantic people, because those mountains may have produced a few individuals near seven feet high. It would be equally absurd to suppose the French are a nation of philosophers, because France has given birth to a Des Cartes, a Maupertuis, a Reaumur, and a Buffon.

I shall not even deny, that the French

LETTER VII.

are by no means deficient in natural capacity; but they are at the same time remarkable for a natural levity, which hinders their youth from cultivating that capacity. This is reinforced by the most preposterous education, and the example of a giddy people, engaged in the most frivolous pursuits. A Frenchman is, by some Jesuit or other monk, taught to read his mother tongue, and to say his prayers in a language he does not understand. He learns to dance and to fence, by the masters of those noble sciences. He becomes a compleat connoisseur in dressing hair, and in adorning his own person, under the hands and instructions of his barber and valet de chambre. If he learns to play upon the flute or the fiddle, he is altogether irresistible. But he piques himself upon being polished above the natives of any other country, by his conversation with the fair sex. In the course of this communication, with which he is indulged from his tender years, he learns like a parrot, by rote, the the whole circle of French compliments, which you know are a set of phrases, ridiculous even to a proverb, and these he throws out indiscriminately to all women, without distinction, in the exercise of that and of address which is here distinguished by the name of gallantry: it is no more than his making love to every woman who will give him the hearing. It is an exercise, by the repetition of which he becomes very pert, very familiar, and very impertinent. Modesty or diffidence, I have already said, is utterly unknown among them, and therefore I wonder there should be a term to express it in their language.

If I was obliged to define politeness, I should call it, The art of making one's self agreeable. I think it an art that necessarily implies a sense of decorum, and a delicacy of sentiment. These are qualities of which (as far as I have been able to observe) a Frenchman has no idea; therefore he never can be deemed polite, except by those persons among whom they are as little understood. His first aim is to adorn his own person with what he calls fine cloaths, that is, the frippery of the fashion. It is no wonder that the heart of a female unimproved by reason, and untinctured with natural good sense, should flutter at the sight of such a gaudy thing, among the number of her admirers: this impression is enforced by fustian compliments, which her own vanity interprets in a literal sense, and still more confirmed by the assiduous attention of the gallant, who, indeed, has nothing else to mind. A Frenchman, in consequence of his mingling with the females from his infancy, not only becomes acquainted with all their customs and

LETTER VII.

mours; but grows wonderfully alert in performing a thousand little offices, which are overlooked by other men, whose time hath been spent in making more valuable acquisitions. He enters, without ceremony, a lady's bed-chamber while she is in bed, reaches her whatever she wants, airs her shift, and helps to put it on. He attends at her toilette, regulates the distribution of her patches, and advises where to lay on the paint. If he visits her when she is dressed, and perceives the least impropriety in her *coeffure*, he insists upon adjusting it with his own hands if he sees a curl, or even a single hair amiss, he produces his comb, his scissars, and pomatum, and sets it to rights with the dexterity of a professed *friseur*. He 'squires her to every place she visits, either on business or pleasure; and, by dedicating his whole time to her, renders himself necessary to her occasions. This I take to be the most agreeable side of his character let us view him on the quarter of impertinence. A Frenchman pries into all your secrets with the most impudent and importunate curiosity, and then discloses them without remorse. If you are indisposed, he questions you about the symptoms of your disorder, with more freedom than your physician would presume to use; very often in the coursest terms. He then proposes his remedy (for they are all quacks,) he prepares it without your knowledge, and worries you with solicitation to take it, without paying the least regard to the opinion of those whom you have chosen to take care of your health. Let you be ever so ill, or averse to company, he forces himself at all times into your bed-chamber; and if it is necessary to give him a peremptory refusal, he is affronted. I have known one of those petite-maitres insist upon paying regular visits twice a day to a poor gentleman who was delirious; and he conversed with him on different subjects, till he was in his last agonies. This attendance is not the effect of attachment or regard, but of meer vanity, that he may afterward boast of his charity and humane disposition though, of all the people I have ever known, I think the French are the least capable of feeling for the distresses of their fellow creatures. Their hearts are not susceptible of deep impressions; and such is their levity, that the imagination has not time to brood long over any disagreeable idea or sensation. As a Frenchman piques himself on his gallantry, he no sooner makes a conquest of a female's heart, than he exposes her character, for the gratification of his vanity. Nay, if he should miscarry in his schemes, he will forge letters and stories to the ruin of the lady's reputation. The

LETTER VII.

is a species of perfidy which one would think should render them odious and detestable to the whole sex; but the case is otherwise. I beg your pardon, Madam; but women are never better pleased than when they see one another exposed; and every individual has such confidence in her own superior charms and discretion, that she thinks she can fix the most volatile, and reform the most treacherous lover.

If a Frenchman is admitted into your family, and distinguished by repeated marks of your friendship and regard, the first return he makes for your civilities is to make love to your wife, if she is handsome; if not, to your sister, or daughter, or niece. If he suffers a repulse from your wife, or attempts in vain to debauch your sister, or your daughter, or your niece, he will, rather than not play the traitor with his gallantry, make his addresses to your grandmother; and ten to one but, in one shape or another, he will find means to ruin the peace of a family in which he has been so kindly entertained. What he cannot accomplish by dint of compliment, and personal attendance, he will endeavour to effect, by reinforcing these with billets-doux, songs and verses, of which he always makes a provision for such purposes. If he is detected in these efforts of treachery, and reproached with his ingratitude, be impudently declares, that what he had done was no more than simple gallantry, considered in France as an indispensible duty on every man who pretended to good breeding. Nay, he will even affirm, that his endeavours to corrupt your wife, or deflower your daughter, were the most genuine proofs he could give of his particular regard for your family.

If a Frenchman is capable of real friendship, it must certainly be the most disagreeable present he can possibly make to a man of a true English character. You know Madam, we are naturally taciturn, soon tired of impertinence, and much subject to fits of disgust. Your French friend intrudes upon you at all hours: he stuns you with his loquacity; he teases you with impertinent questions about your domestic and private affairs; he attempts to meddle in all your concerns; and forces his advice upon you with the most unwearied importunity. he asks the price of every thing you wear, and, so sure as you tell him, undervalues it, without hesitation: he affirms it is in a bad taste, ill-contrived, ill-made; that you have been imposed upon both with respect to the fashion and the price, that the marquis of this, or the countess of that, has one that is perfectly elegant, quite in the *bon ton*, and yet it cost her little more than you gave for a thing that no body would wear.

If there were five hundred dishes at table, a Frenchman will eat of all of them, and then complain he has no appetite. This I have several times remarked. A friend of mine gained a considerable wager upon an experiment of this kind: the petit maitre ate of fourteen different *plats*, besides the desart; then disparaged the cook, declaring he was no better than a *marmiton*, or turn-spit.

The French have a most ridiculous fondness for their hair, and this I believe they inherit from their remote ancestors. The first race of French kings were distinguished by their long hair, and certainly the people of this country consider it as an indispensible ornament. A Frenchman will sooner part with his religion than with his hair, which, indeed, no consideration will induce him to forego. I know a gentleman afflicted with a continual head-ach, and a defluxion on his eyes, who was told by his physician that the best chance he had of being cured would be to have his head close shaved, and bathed every day in cold water. "How, (cried he,) cut my hair? ah Doctor, your most humble servant!" He dismissed his physician, lost his eye-sight, and almost his senses, and is now led about with his hair in a bag, and a piece of green silk hanging like a screen before his face. Count Saxe, and other military writers have demonstrated the absurdity of a soldier's wearing a long head of hair; nevertheless every soldier in this country wears a long queue, which makes a delicate mark on his white cloathing; and this ridiculous foppery has descended even to the lowest class of people. The *decrotteur*, who cleans your shoes at the corner of the Pont Neuf, has a tail of this kind hanging down to his rump; and even the peasant who drives an ass loaded with dung, wears his hair *en queue*, though, perhaps, he has neither shirt nor breeches. This is the ornament upon which he bestows much time and pains, and in the exhibition of which he finds full gratification for his vanity. Considering the harsh features of the common people in this country, their diminutive stature, their grimaces, and that long appendage, they have no small resemblance to large baboons walking upright; and perhaps this similitude has helped to entail upon them the ridicule of their neighbours.

A French friend tires out your patience with long visits; and, far from taking the most palpable hints to withdraw when he perceives you uneasy, observes you are low spirited, and therefore he declares he will keep you company. This perseverance shews that he must either be void of all pe-

[penetration], or that his disposition must be [tr]uly diabolical. Rather than be tormented [w]ith such a fiend, a man had better turn [h]im out of doors, even though at the ha[z]ard of being run through the body.

The French are generally counted insin[c]ere, and taxed with want of generosity. [B]ut I think these reproaches are not well [f]ounded. High flown professions of friend[sh]ip and attachment constitute the language [o]f common compliment in this country, [a]nd are never supposed to be understood in [t]he literal acceptation of the words; and, [i]f their acts of generosity are but very [r]are, we ought to ascribe that rarity, not [s]o much to a deficiency of generous senti[m]ents, as to their vanity and ostentation, [w]hich engrossing all their funds, utterly [d]isable them from exerting the virtues of [b]eneficence. Vanity, indeed, predominates [a]mong all ranks to such a degree, that they [ar]e the greatest *egotists* in the world; and [t]he most insignificant individual talks in com[p]any with the same conceit and arrogance [a]s a person of the greatest importance. [N]either conscious poverty nor disgrace will [r]estrain him in the least either from a[ss]uming his full share of the conversation, [o]r making his addresses to the finest lady, [w]hom he has the smallest opportunity to [ap]proach: nor is he restrained by any o[th]er consideration whatsoever. It is all one to him whether he himself has a wife of his own, or the lady a husband; whether she is designed for the cloister, or pre-ingaged to his best friend and benefactor. He takes it for granted that his addresses cannot but be acceptable; and, if he meets with a repulse, he condemns her taste, but never doubts his own qualifications.

I have a great many things to say of their military character, and their punctilios of honour, which last are equally absurd and pernicious, but as this letter has run to an unconscionable length, I shall defer them till another opportunity. Mean-while I have the honour to be, with very particular esteem,

Madam,

Your most obedient servant.

LETTER VIII.

To Mr M———.

Lyons, October 19.

DEAR SIR,

I Was favoured with yours at Paris, and look upon your reproaches as the proof

LETTER VIII.

of your friendship. The truth is, I considered all the letters I have hitherto written on the subject of my travels, as written to your society in general, though they have been addressed to one individual of it; and if they contain any thing that can either amuse or inform, I desire that henceforth all I send may be freely perused by all the members.

With respect to my health, about which you so kindly inquire, I have nothing new to communicate. I had reason to think that my bathing in the sea at Boulogne produced a good effect, in strengthening my relaxed fibres. You know how subject I was to colds in England; that I could not stir abroad after sun-set, nor expose myself to the smallest damp, nor walk till the least moisture appeared on my skin, without being laid up for ten days or a fortnight. At Paris, however, I went out every day, with my hat under my arm, though the weather was wet and cold. I walked in the garden at Versailles even after it was dark, with my head uncovered, on a cold evening, when the ground was far from being dry; nay, at Marli, I sauntered above a mile through damp alleys, and wet grass: and from none of these risques did I feel the least inconvenience.

In one of our excursions we visited the manufacture for porcelain, which the king of France has established at the village of St Cloud, on the road to Versailles, and which is, indeed, a noble monument of his munificence. It is a very large building, both commodious and magnificent, where a great number of artists are employed, and where this elegant superfluity is carried to as great perfection as it ever was at Dresden. Yet, after all, I know not whether the porcelain made at Chelsea may not vie with the productions either of Dresden or St Cloud. If it falls short of either, it is not in the design, painting, enamel, or other ornaments, but only in the composition of the metal, and the method of managing it in the furnace. Our porcelain seems to be a partial vitrification of levigated flint and fine pipe clay, mixed together in a certain proportion; and if the pieces are not removed from the fire in the very critical moment, they will be either too little, or too much vitrified. In the first case, I apprehend they will not acquire a proper degree of cohesion; they will be apt to be corroded, discoloured, and to crumble, like the first essays that were made at Chelsea. In the second case, they will be little better than imperfect glass.

There are three methods of travelling from Paris to Lyons, which, by the short post road, is a journey of about three hundred and sixty miles. One is by the *gence*, or stage-coach, which performs it in five days; and every passenger pays one hundred livres, in consideration of which, he not only has a seat in the carriage, but is maintained on the road. The inconveniences attending this way of travelling are these: you are crouded into the carriage, to the number of eight persons, so as to sit very uneasy, and sometimes run the risque of being stifled among very indifferent company. You are hurried out of bed, at four, three, nay often at two o'clock in the morning. You are obliged to eat in the French way, which is very disagreeable to an English palate; and at Chalons you must embark upon the Soane, in a boat which conveys you to Lyons, so that the two last days of your journey are by water. All these were insurmountable objections to me, who am in such a bad state of health, troubled with an asthmatic cough, spitting, slow fever, and restlessness, which demands a continual change of place, as well as free air, and room for motion. I was this day visited by two young gentlemen, sons of Mr Guastaldi, late minister from Genoa at London. I had seen them at Paris, at the house of the Duchess of Douglas. They came hither, with their conductor, in the *diligence*; and assured me, that nothing could be more disagreeable than their situation in that carriage.

LETTER VIII.

Another way of travelling in this country is to hire a coach and four horses; and this method I was inclined to take: but when I went to the bureau, where alone these voitures are to be had, I was given to understand, that it would cost me six and twenty guineas, and travel so slow that I should be ten days upon the road. These carriages are let by the same persons who farm the diligence; and for this they have an exclusive privilege, which makes them very saucy and insolent. When I mentioned my servant, they gave me to understand that I must pay two loui'dores more for his seat on the coach-box. As I could not relish these terms, nor brook the thoughts of being so long upon the road, I had recourse to the third method, which is going post.

In England you know I should have had nothing to do, but to hire a couple of post-chaises from stage to stage, with two horses in each; but here the case is quite otherwise. The post is farmed from the king, who lays travellers under contribution for his own benefit, and has published a set of oppressive ordonnances, which no stranger nor native dares transgress. The postmaster finds nothing but horses and guides the carriage you yourself must provide. If there are four persons within the carriage, you are obliged to have six horses, and two postilions; and if your servant sits on the outside, either before or behind, you must pay for a seventh. You pay double for the first stage from Paris, and twice double for passing through Fontainbleau when the court is there, as well as at coming to Lyons, and at leaving this city. These are called royal posts, and are undoubtedly a scandalous imposition.

There are two post-roads from Paris to Lyons, one of sixty-five posts, by the way of Moulins; the other of fifty-nine, by the way of Dijon in Burgundy. This last I chose, partly to save sixty livres, and partly to see the wine harvest of Burgundy, which, I was told, was a season of mirth and jollity among all ranks of people. I hired a very good coach for ten louis'dores to Lyons, and set out from Paris on the thirteenth instant, with six horses, two postilions, and my own servant on horseback. We made no stop at Fontainbleau, though the court was there; but lay at Moret, which is one stage further, a very paltry little town; where, however, we found good accommodation. I shall not pretend to describe the castle or palace of Fontainbleau, of which I had only a glimpse in passing; but the forest, in the middle of which it stands, is a noble chace of great extent, beautifully wild and romantic, well stored with game of all forts, and abounding with excellent timber. It put me in mind of the New Forest in Hampshire; but the hills, rocks, and mountains, with which it is diversified, render it more agreeable.

The people of this country dine at noon, and travellers always find an ordinary prepared at every *auberge*, or public-house, on the road. Here they sit down promiscuously, and dine at so much a head. The usual price is thirty sols for dinner, and forty for supper, including lodging; for this moderate expence they have two courses and a desert. If you eat in your own apartment, you pay, instead of forty sols, three, and in some places, four livres a head. I and my family could not well dispense with our tea and toast in the morning, and had no stomach to eat at noon. For my own part, I hate the French cookery, and abominate garlic, with which all their ragouts, in this part of the country, are highly seasoned: we therefore formed a different plan of living upon the road. Before we left Paris, we laid in a stock of tea, chocolate, cured neats tongues, and *saucissons* or Bologna sausages, both of which we found in great perfection in that capital, where, indeed, there are excellent provisions of all sorts. About ten in the morning we stopped to breakfast at some auberge, where we always found bread, butter, and milk. In the mean time we ordered a *poulard* or two to be roasted; and these, wrapped in a napkin, were put into the boot of the coach, together with bread, wine, and water. About two or three in the afternoon, while the horses were changing, we laid a cloth upon our knees, and producing our store, with a few earthern plates, discussed our short meal without further ceremony. This was followed by a desert of grapes and other fruit, which we had also provided. I must own I found these transient refreshments much more agreeable than any regular meal I ate upon the road. The wine commonly used in Burgundy is so weak and thin, that you would not drink it in England. The very best which they sell at Dijon, the capital of this province, for three livres a bottle, is in strength, and even in flavour, greatly inferior to what I have drank in London. I believe all the first growth is either consumed in the house of the noblesse, or sent abroad to foreign markets. I have drank excellent Burgundy at Brussels for a florin a bottle; that is, little more than twenty pence sterling.

The country from the forest of Fontainbleau to the Lyonnois, through which we passed, is rather agreeable than fertile, being part of Champagne and the duchy of Burgundy, watered by three pleasant pastoral rivers, the Seine, the Yonne, and the Soane. The flat country is laid out chiefly for corn; but produces more rye than wheat. Almost all the ground seems to be ploughed up, so that there is little or nothing lying fallow. There are very few inclosures, scarce any meadow ground, and, so far as I could observe, a great scarcity of cattle. We sometimes found it very difficult to procure half a pint of milk for our tea. In Burgundy I saw a peasant ploughing the ground with a jack-ass, a lean cow, and a he-goat, yoked together. It is generally observed, that a great number of black cattle are bred and fed on the mountains of Burgundy, which are the highest lands in France; but I saw very few. The peasants in France are so wretchedly poor, and so much oppressed by their landlords, that they cannot afford to inclose their grounds, or give a proper respite to their lands; or to stock their farms with a sufficient number of black cattle to produce the necessary manure, without which agriculture can never be carried to any degree of perfection. Indeed, whatever efforts a few individuals may make for the benefit of their own estates, husbandry in France will never be

LETTER VIII.

generally improved, until the farmer is free and independent.

From the frequency of towns and villages, I should imagine this country is very populous; yet it must be owned that the towns are in general thinly inhabited. I saw a good number of country seats and plantations near the banks of the rivers on each side; and a great many convents, sweetly situated, on rising grounds, where the air is most pure, and the prospect most agreeable. It is surprising to see how happy the founders of those religious houses have been in their choice of situations, all the world over.

In passing through this country I was very much struck with the sight of large ripe clusters of grapes, entwined with the briars and thorns of common hedges on the way-side. The mountains of Burgundy are covered with vines from the bottom to the top, and seem to be raised by nature on purpose to extend the surface, and to expose it the more advantageously to the rays of the sun. The *vandange* was but just begun, and the people were employed in gathering the grapes, but I saw no signs of festivity among them. Perhaps their joy was a little damped by the bad prospect of their harvest; for they complained that the weather had been so unfavourable as to hinder the grapes from ripening. I thought, indeed, there was something uncomfortable in seeing the vintage thus retarded till the beginning of winter for, in some parts, I found the weather extremely cold; particularly at a place called *Maison-neuve*, where we lay, there was a hard frost, and in the morning the pools were covered with a thick crust of ice. My personal adventures on the road were such as will not bear a recital. They consisted of petty disputes with landladies, post-masters and postilions. The highways seem to be perfectly safe. We did not find that any robberies were ever committed, although we did not see one of the *marechausse* from Paris to Lyons. You know the *marechausse* are a body of troopers well mounted, maintained in France as safe-guards to the public roads. It is a reproach upon England that some such patrol is not appointed for the protection of travellers.

At Sens in Champaigne, my servant, who had rode on before to bespeak fresh horses, told me, that the domestic of another company had been provided before him, although it was not his turn, as he had arrived later at the post. Provoked at this partiality, I resolved to chide the post-master, and accordingly addressed myself to a person who stood at the door of the auberge. He was a jolly figure, fat and fair, dressed in an odd kind of garb, with a gold-laced cap on his head, and a cambric handkerchief pinned to his middle. The sight of such a fantastic petit maitre, in the character of a post-master, increased my spleen. I called to him, with an air of authority, mixed with indignation, and when he came up to the coach, asked, in a peremptory tone, if he did not understand the king's ordonnance concerning the regulation of posts? He laid his hand upon his breast; but before he could make any answer, I pulled out the post-book, and began to read, with great vociferation, the article which orders, that the traveller who comes first shall be first served. By this time the fresh horses being put to the carriage, and the postilions mounted, the coach set off all on a sudden, with uncommon speed. I imagined the post-master had given the fellows a signal to be gone, and, in this persuasion, thrusting my head out at the window, I bestowed some epithets upon him, which must have sounded very harsh in the ears of a Frenchman. We stopped for a refreshment at a little town called *Torgne-ville*, where (by the bye) I was scandalously imposed upon, and even abused, by a virago of a landlady. Then proceeding to the next stage, I was given to understand we could not be supplied with fresh horses. Here I perceived at the door of the inn the same person whom I had reproached at Sens. He came up to the coach, and told me, that notwithstanding what the guides had said, I should have fresh horses in a few minutes. I imagined he was master both of this house and the auberge at Sens, between which he passed and repassed occasionally; and that he was now desirous of making me amends for the affront he had put upon me at the other place. Observing that one of the trunks behind was a little displaced, he assisted my servant in adjusting it: then he entered into conversation with me, and gave me to understand, that in a post-chaise, which we had passed, was an English gentleman on his return from Italy. I wanted to know who he was, and when he said he could not tell, I asked him, in a very abrupt manner, why he had not inquired of his servant. He shrugged up his shoulders, and retired to the inn door. Having waited about half an hour, I beckoned to him, and when he approached upbraided him with having told me that should be supplied with fresh horses in few minutes. he seemed shocked, and answered, that he thought he had reason for what he said, observing, that it was as disagreeable to him as to me to wait for relay. As it began to rain, I pulled u the glass in his face, and he withdrew again to the door, seemingly ruffled at my deportment. In a little time the horses arrived, and three of them were immediately put to a very handsome post-chaise, into which he stepped, and set out, accompanied by a man in a rich livery on horseback. Astonished at this circumstance, I asked the hostler who he was, and he replied, that he was a man of fashion (un seigneur) who lived in the neighbourhood of Auxerre. I was much mortified to find that I had treated a nobleman so scurvily, and scolded my own people for not having more penetration than myself. I dare say he did not fail to descant upon the brutal behaviour of the Englishman; and that my mistake served with him to confirm the national reproach of bluntness and ill breeding, under which we lye in this country. The truth is, I was that day more than usually peevish, from the bad weather, as well as from the dread of a fit of the asthma, with which I was threatned: and I dare say my appearance seemed as uncouth to him, as his travelling dress appeared to me. I had a grey mourning frock under a wide great coat, a bob wig without powder, a very large laced hat, and a meagre, wrinkled, discontented countenance.

The fourth night of our journey we lay

VOL. I. L.

at Macon, and the next day paſſed through the Lyonnois, which is a fine country, full of towns, villages, and gentlemen's houſes. In paſſing through the Maconnois, we ſaw a great many fields of Indian corn, which grows to the height of ſix or ſeven feet: it is made into flour for the uſe of the common people, and goes by the name of *Turkey wheat*. Here likewiſe, as well as in Dauphine, they raiſe a vaſt quantity of very large pompions, with the contents of which they thicken their ſoup and ragouts.

As we travelled only while the ſun was up, on account of my ill health, and the poſt horſes in France are in bad order, we ſeldom exceeded twenty leagues a-day.

I was directed to a lodging-houſe at Lyons, which being full, they ſhewed us to a tavern, where I was led up three pair of ſtairs, to an apartment conſiſting of three paltry chambers, for which the people demanded twelve livres a-day: for dinner and ſupper they aſked thirty-two, beſides three livres for my ſervant, ſo that my daily expence would have amounted to about forty-ſeven livres, excluſive of breakfaſt and coffee in the afternoon. I was ſo provoked at this extortion, that without anſwering one word, I drove to another auberge, where I now am, and pay at the rate of two-and-thirty livres a-day, for which I am very badly lodged, and but very indifferently entertained. I mention these circumstances to give you an idea of the imposition to which strangers are subject in this country. It must be owned, however, that in the article of eating, I might save half the money by going to the public ordinary; but this is a scheme of œconomy which (exclusive of other disagreeable circumstances) neither my own health, nor that of my wife permits me to embrace. My journey from Paris to Lyons, including the hire of the coach, and all expences on the road, has cost me, within a few shillings, forty lou'dores. From Paris our baggage (though not plombé) was not once examined till we arrived in this city, at the gate of which we were questioned by one of the searchers, who, being tipt with half a crown, allowed us to proceed without further inquiry.

I purposed to stay in Lyons until I should receive some letters I expected from London, to be forwarded by my banker at Paris: but the enormous expence of living in this manner has determined me to set out in a day or two for Montpelier, although that place is a good way out of the road to Nice. My reasons for taking that rout I shall communicate in my next. Mean-while, I am ever,

Dear Sir,

Your affectionate
and obliged humble servant.

LETTER IX.

Montpelier, November 5 1763.

DEAR SIR,

THE city of Lyons has been so often and so circumstantially described, that I cannot pretend to say any thing new on the subject. Indeed I know very little of it, but what I have read in books, as I had but one day to make a tour of the streets, squares, and other remarkable places. The bridge over the Rhone seems to be so slightly built, that I should imagine it would be one day carried away by that rapid river; especially as the arches are so small, that, after great rains, they are sometimes *bouchees*, or stopped up; that is, they do not admit a sufficient passage for the increased body of the water. In order to remedy this defect in some measure, they found an artist some years ago, who has removed a middle pier, and thrown two arches into one. This alteration they looked upon as a masterpiece in architecture, though there is many a common mason in England who would have undertaken and performed the work, without valuing himself much upon the enterprize. This bridge, no more than that of St Esprit, is built, not in a strait line across the river, but with a curve, which forms a convexity to oppose the current. Such a bend is certainly calculated for the better resisting the general impetuosity of the stream, and has no bad effect to the eye.

Lyons is a great, populous, and flourishing city; but I am surprised to find it is counted a healthy place, and that the air of it is esteemed favourable to pulmonic disorders. It is situated on the confluence of two large rivers, from which there must be a great evaporation, as well as from the low marshy grounds which these rivers often overflow. This must render the air moist, frouzy, and even putrid, if it was not well ventilated by winds from the mountains of Swisserland; and in the latter-end of autumn it must be subject to fogs. The morning we set out from thence, the whole city and adjacent plains were covered with so thick a fog, that we could not distinguish from the coach the head of the foremost mule that drew it. Lyons is said to be very hot in summer, and very cold in winter; therefore I imagine must abound with inflammatory and intermittent disorders in the spring and fall of the year.

My reasons for going to Montpelier, which is out of the strait road to Nice, were these. Having no acquaintance nor correspondents in the South of France, I had desired my credit might be sent to the same house to which my heavy baggage was consigned. I expected to find my baggage at Cette, which is the sea port of Montpelier; and there I also hoped to find a vessel, in which I might be transported by sea to Nice, without further trouble. I longed to try what effect the boasted air of Montpelier would have upon my constitution; and I had a great desire to see the famous monuments of antiquity in and about the ancient city of Nismes, which is about eight leagues short of Montpelier.

At the inn where we lodged I found return berlin, belonging to Avignon, with three mules, which are the animals commonly used for carriages in this country. This I hired for five lou'dores. The coach was large, commodious, and well fitted; the mules were strong and in good order; and the driver whose name was Joseph, appeared to be a sober, sagacious, intelligent fellow, perfectly well acquainted ed with every place in the South of France. He told me he was owner of the coach: but I afterwards learned he was no other than a hired servant. I likewise detected him in some knavery, in the course of our journey; and plainly perceived he had a fellow-feeling with the inkeepers on the road; but, in other respects, he was very obliging, serviceable, and even entertaining. There are some knavish practices of this kind, at which a traveller will do well to shut his eyes, for his own ease and convenience. He will be lucky if he has to do with a sensible knave, like Joseph, who understood his interest too well to be guilty of very flagrant pieces of imposition.

A man impatient to be at his journey's end, will find this a most disagreeable way of travelling. In summer it must be quite intolerable. The mules are very sure, but very slow. The journey seldom exceeds eight leagues, about four and twenty miles a day: and as those people have certain fixed stages, you are sometimes obliged to rise in a morning before day; a circumstance very grievous to persons in ill health. These inconveniences, however, were over-balanced by other agreemens. We no sooner quitted Lyons than we got into summer weather; and travelling through a most romantic country, along the banks of the Rhone, had opportunities (from the flowness of our pace) to contemplate its beauties at leisure.

The rapidity of the Rhone is, in a great measure, owing to its being confined within steep banks on each side. These are formed, almost through its whole course, by a double chain of mountains, which rise with an abrupt ascent from both banks of the river. The mountains are covered with vineyards, interspersed with small summer-houses, and in many places they are crowned with churches, chapels, and convents, which add greatly to the romantic beauty of the prospect. The highroad, as far as Avignon, lyes along the side of the river, which runs almost in a straight line, and affords great convenience for inland commerce. Travellers bound to the southern parts of France, generally embark in the *coche d'eau* at Lyons, and glide down this river with great velocity, passing a great number of towns and villages, on each side, where they find ordinaries every day at dinner and supper. In good weather there is no danger in this method of travelling, 'till you come to the Pont St Esprit, where the stream runs through the arches with such rapidity, that the boat is sometimes overset. But those passengers who are under any apprehension are landed above bridge

LETTER IX.

and taken in again after the boat has paſſed, juſt in the ſame manner as at London
Bridge. The boats that go up the river
are drawn againſt the ſtream by oxen, which
ſwim through one of the arches of this
bridge, the driver ſitting between the horns
of the foremoſt beaſt. We ſet out from
Lyons early on Monday morning: and as
a robbery had been a few days before committed in that neighbourhood, I ordered
my ſervant to load my muſquetoon with a
charge of eight balls. By the bye, this
piece did not fail to attract the curioſity
and admiration of the people in every
place through which we paſſed. The carriage no ſooner halted, than a crowd immediately ſurrounded the man to view the
blunderbuſs, which they dignified with the
title of *petit canon*. At Nuys in Burgundy he fired it in the air, and the whole
mob diſperſed, and ſcampered off like a
flock of ſheep. In our journey hither, we
generally ſet out in a morning at eight o'
clock, and travelled 'till noon, when the
mules were put up and reſted a couple of
hours. During this halt Joſeph went to
dinner and we went to breakfaſt, after
which we ordered proviſion for our re-
freſhment in the coach, which we took
about three or four in the afternoon, halt-
ing for that purpoſe by the ſide of ſome
tranſparent brook, which afforded excel-

lent water to mix with our wine. In this country I was almost poisoned with garlic, which they mix in their ragouts, and all their sauces; nay, the smell of it perfumes the very chambers, as well as every person you approach. I was also very sick of *beca ficas, grieves,* and other little birds, which are served up twice a day at all ordinaries on the road. They make their appearance in vine leaves, and are always half raw, in which condition the French chuse to eat them, rather than run the risque of losing the juice by over-roasting.

The peasants on the South of France are poorly clad, and look as if they were half starved, diminutive, fraitly, and meagre; and yet the common people who travel, live luxuriously on the road. Every carrier and mule driver has two meals a-day, consisting each of a couple of courses and a desert, with tollerable small wine. —That which is called *hermitage*, and grows in this province of Dauphine, is sold on the spot for three livres a bottle. The common draught which you have at meals in this country, is remarkably strong, tho' in flavour much inferior to that of Burgundy. The accommodation is tolerable, though they demand (even in this cheap country) the exorbitant price of four livres a head for every meal, of those who chuse to eat in their own apartments I infifted, however, upon paying them with three, which they received, though not without murmuring and feeming difcontented. In this journey we found plenty of good mutton, pork, and poultry, and game, including the red partridge, which is near twice as big as the partridge of England. Their hares are likewife furprifingly large and juicy. We faw great flocks of black turkeys feeding in the fields, but no black cattle; and milk was fo fcarce, that sometimes we were obliged to drink our tea without it.

One day perceiving a meadow on the fide of the road full of a flower which I took to be the crocus, I defired my fervant to alight and pull fome of them. He delivered the mufquetoon to Jofeph, who began to tamper with it, and off it went with a prodigious report, augmented by an eccho from the mountains that fkirted the road. The mules were fo frightened, that they went off at the gallop; and Jofeph, for fome minutes, could neither manage the reins, nor open his mouth. At length he recollected himfelf, and the cattle were ftopt, by the affiftance of the fervant, to whom he delivered the mufquetoon, with a fignificant fhake of the head. Then alighting from the box, he examined the heads of his three mules, and kiffed each of them in his turn. Finding they had received no damage, he came up to the coach, with a pale visage, and staring eyes, and said it was God's mercy he had not killed his beasts. I answered, that it was a greater mercy he had not killed his passengers; for the muzzle of the piece might have been directed our way as well as any other, and in that case Joseph might have been hanged for murder. "I had as good be hanged (said he) for murder, as be ruined by the loss of my cattle." This adventure made such an impression upon him, that he recounted it to every person we met; nor would he ever touch the blunderbuss from that day. I was often diverted with the conversation of this fellow, who was very arch and very communicative. Every afternoon he used to stand upon the foot-board, at the side of the coach, and discourse with us an hour together. Passing by the gibbet of Valencia, which stands very near the high road, we saw one body hanging quite naked, and another lying broken on the wheel. I recollected that Mandrin had suffered in that place, and calling to Joseph to mount the foot-board, asked if he had ever seen that famous adventurer. At mention of the name of Mandrin, the tear started in Joseph's eye, he discharged a deep sigh, or rather groan, and told me he was his dear friend. I was a little startled at this declaration; however, I concealed my thoughts, and began to aſk queſtions about the character and exploits of a man who had made ſuch noiſe in the world.

He told me, Mandrin was a native of Valencia, of mean extraction. that he had ſerved as a ſoldier in the army, and afterwards acted as *maltotier*, or tax-gatherer: that at length he turned *contrebandier*, or ſmuggler, and by his ſuperior qualities raiſed himſelf to the command of a formidable gang, conſiſting of five hundred perſons well armed with carbines and piſtols. He had fifty horſe for his troopers, and three hundred mules for the carriage of his merchandize. His head quarters were in Savoy: but he made incurſions into Dauphine, and ſet the *marechauſſee* at defiance. He maintained ſeveral bloody ſkirmiſhes with theſe troopers, as well as with other regular detachments, and in all thoſe actions ſignalized himſelf by his courage and conduct. Coming up at one time with fifty of the *marechauſſee*, who were in queſt of him, he told them very calmly, he had occaſion for their horſes and acoutrements, and deſired them to diſmount. At that inſtant his gang appeared, and the troopers complied with his requeſt, without making the leaſt oppoſition. Joſeph ſaid he was as generous as he was brave, and never moleſted travellers, nor did the leaſt injury to the poor; but, on the contrary, relieved them very often. He used to oblige the gentlemen in the country to take his merchandize, his tobacco, brandy, and muslins, at his own price; and in the same manner he laid the open towns under contribution. When he had no merchandise, he borrowed money of them upon the credit of what he should bring when he was better provided. He was at last betrayed, by his wench, to the colonel of a French regiment, who went with a detachment in the night to the place where he lay in Savoy, and surprised him in a wood house, while his people were absent in different parts of the country. For this intrusion, the court of France made an apology to the king of Sardinia, in whose territories he was taken. Mandrin being conveyed to Valencia, his native place, was for some time permitted to go abroad, under a strong guard, with chains upon his legs; and here he conversed freely with all sorts of people, flattering himself with the hopes of a pardon, in which, however, he was disappointed. An order came from court to bring him to his trial, when he was found guilty, and condemned to be broke on the wheel. Joseph said he drank a bottle of wine with him the night before his execution. He bore his fate with great resolution, observing, that if the letter which h had written to the King had been delivered, he certainly should have obtained his Majesty's pardon. His executioner was one of his own gang, who was pardoned on condition of performing this office. You know that criminals broke upon the wheel are first strangled, unless the sentence imports that they shall be broke alive. As Mandrin had not been guilty of cruelty in the course of his delinquency, he was indulged with this favour. Speaking to the executioner, whom he had formerly commanded, " Joseph, (dit il) je ne veux pas que tu me touche, jusqu'a ce que je sois froid mort." Joseph, said he, thou shalt not touch me till I am quite dead —Our driver had no sooner pronounced these words, than I was struck with a suspicion that he himself was the executioner of his friend Mandrin. On that suspicion I exclaimed, " Ah! ah! Joseph!" The fellow blushed up to the eyes, and said, *Oui, son nom etoit Joseph aussi bien que le mien.* I did not think proper to prosecute the inquiry; but did not much relish the nature of Joseph's connections. The truth is, he had very much the looks of a ruffian; though, I must own, his behaviour was very obliging and submissive.

On the fifth day of our journey, in the morning we passed the famous bridge at St Esprit, which to be sure is a great curiosity, from its length, and the number of its arches: but these arches are too small, the passage above is too narrow; and the whole appears to be too slight, considering the force and impetuosity of the river. It is not comparable to the bridge at Westminster, either for beauty or solidity. Here we entered Languedoc, and were stopped to have our baggage examined: but the searcher being tipped with a three livre piece, allowed it to pass.—Before we leave Dauphine, I must observe, that I was not a little surprized to see figs and chesnuts growing in the open fields, at the discretion of every passenger. It was this day I saw the famous Pont du Garde: but as I cannot possibly include, in this letter, a description of that beautiful bridge, and of the other antiquities belonging to Nismes, I will defer it till the next opportunity being, in the mean time, with equal truth and affection,

  Dear Sir,

   Your obliged humble servant.

LETTER X.

Montpellier, November 10 1763

DEAR SIR,

BY the Pont St Esprit we entered the province of Languedoc, and breakfasted at Bagnole, which is a little paltry town; from whence, however, there is an excellent road through a mountain, made at a great expence, and extending about four leagues. About five in the afternoon, I had the first glimpse of the famous Pont du Guarde, which stands on the right hand, about the distance of a league from the post road to Nismes, and about three leagues from that city. I would not willingly pass for a false enthusiast in taste; but I cannot help observing, that from the first distant view of this noble monument, till we came near enough to see it perfectly, I felt the strongest emotions of impatience that I had ever known; and obliged our driver to put his mules to the full gallop, in the apprehension that it would be dark before we reached the place. I expected to find the building, in some measure, ruinous; but was agreeably disappointed, to see it look as fresh as the bridge at Westminster. The climate is either so pure and dry, or the freestone, with which it is built, so hard, that the very angles of them remain as acute as if they had been cut last year. Indeed, some large stones have dropped out of the arches; but the whole is admirably preserved, and presents the eye with a piece of architecture so unaffectedly elegant, so simple and majestic, that I will defy the most phlegmatic and stupid spectator to behold it without admiration. It was raised in the Augustan age, by the Roman colony of Nismes, to convey a stream of water between two mountains, for the use of that city. It stands over the river Gardon, which is a beautiful pastoral stream, brawling among rocks, which form a number of pretty natural cascades, and overshadowed on each side with trees and shrubs, which greatly add to the rural beauties of the scene. It rises in the Cevennes, and the sand of it produces gold, as we learn from Mr Reaumur, in his essay on this subject, inserted in the French Memoirs for the year 1718.———If I lived at Nismes, or Avignon (which last city is within four short leagues of it) I should take pleasure in forming parties to come hither, in summer to dine under one of the arches of the Pont du Garde, on a cold collation.

This work consists of three bridges, or tire of arches, one above another; the first of six, the second of eleven, and the third of thirty-six. The height, comprehending the aqueduct on the top, amounts to 174 feet three inches the length between the two mountains which it unites, extends to 723. The order of architecture is the Tuscan. but the symmetry of it is inconceiveable. By scooping the bases of the pilasters of the second tire of arches, they had made a passage for foot-travellers: but though the Ancients far excelled us in beauty, they certainly fell short of the Moderns in point of conveniency. The citizens of Avignon have, in this particular, improved the Roman work with a new bridge by apposition, constructed on the same plan with that of the lower tire of arches, of which indeed it seems to be a part, affording a broad and commodious passage over the river, to horses and carriages of all kinds. The aqueduct, for the continuance of which this superb work was raised, conveyed a stream of sweet water from the fountain of Eure, near the city of Uzes, and extended near six leagues in length.

In approaching Nismes, you see the ruins of a Roman tower, built on the summit of a hill which over-looks the city. It seems to have been intended, at first, as a watch, or signal-tower, though, in the sequel, it was used as a fortress. what remains of it is about ninety feet high; the architecture of the Doric order. I no sooner alighted at the inn, than I was presented with a pamphlet, containing an account of Nismes and its antiquities, which every stranger buys. There are persons too who attend in order to shew the town, and you will always be accosted by some shabby antiquarian, who presents you with medals for sale, assuring you they are genuine antiques, and were dug out of the ruins of the Roman temple and baths. All those fellows are cheats, and they have often laid under contribution raw English travellers, who had more money than discretion. To such they sell the vilest and most common trash but when they meet with a connoisseur, they produce some medals which are really valuable and curious.

Nismes, anciently called *Nemausis*, was originally a colony of Romans, settled by Augustus Cæsar, after the battle of Actium. It is still of considerable extent, and said to contain twelve thousand families; but the number seems by this account to be greatly exaggerated. Certain it is, the city must have been formerly very extensive, as appears from the circuit of the ancient walls, the remains of which are still to be seen. Its present size is not one third of its former extent. Its temples baths, statues, towers, basilica, and amphitheatre, prove it to have been a city of great opulence and magnificence. At present, the remains of these antiquities are all that make it respectable or remarkable; though here are manufactures of silk and wool carried on with good success. The water necessary for these works is supplied by a source at the foot of the rock, upon which the tower is placed; and here were discovered the ruins of Roman baths, which had been formed and adorned with equal taste and magnificence. Among the rubbish they found a vast profusion of columns, vases, capitals, cornices, inscriptions, medals, statues, and, among other things, the finger of a colossal statue in bronze, which, according to the rules of proportion, must have been fifteen feet high. From these particulars, it appears that the edifices must have been spacious and magnificent. Part of a tesselated pavement still remains. The anient pavement of the bath is still entire; all the rubbish has been cleared away; and the baths, in a great measure, restored on the old plan, though they are not at present used for any thing but ornament. The water is collected into two vast reservoirs, and a canal built and lined with hewn stone. There are three handsome bridges thrown over this vast canal. It contains a great body of excellent water, which by pipes and other small branching canals, traverses the town, and is converted to many different purposes of œconomy and manufacture. Between the Roman bath and these great canals, the ground is agreeably laid out in pleasure walks, for the recreation of the inhabitants. Here are likewise ornaments of architecture, which favour much more of French foppery than of the simplicity and greatness of the ancients. It is very surprizing that this fountain should produce such a great body of water as fills the basin of the source, the Roman basin, two large deep canals three hundred feet in length, two vast basins that make part of the great canal, which is eighteen hundred feet long, eighteen feet deep, and forty eight feet broad. When I saw it, there was in it about eight or nine feet of water, transparent as crystal. It must be observed, however, for the honour of French cleanliness, that in the Roman basin through which this noble stream of water passes, I perceived two washermen at work upon children's clouts and dirty linen. Surprized and much disgusted at this filthy phænomenon, I asked by what means, and by whose permission those dirty hags had got down into the basin, in order to contaminate the water at its fountain-head; and understood the belonged to the commandant of the place, who had the keys of the subterranean passage.

Fronting the Roman baths are the ruins of an ancient temple, which according to tradition, was dedicated to Diana: but it has been observed by connoisseurs, that all the ancient temples of this goddess were of the Ionic order; whereas this is partly Corinthian, and partly composite. It is about seventy foot long, and six and thirty in breadth, arched above, and built of large blocks of stone, joined together without any cement. The walls are still standing, with three great tabernacles at the further end, fronting the entrance. On each side there are niches in the intercolumniation of the walls, together with pedestals and shafts of pillars, cornices, and an entablature, which indicate the former magnificence of the building. It was destroyed during the civil war that raged in the reign of Henry III. of France.

It is amazing, that the successive irruptions of barbarous nations; of Goths, Vandals, and Moors; of fanatic croisards, still more sanguinary and illiberal than those Barbarians, should have spared this temple, as well as two other still more noble monuments of architecture, that to this day adorn the city of Nismes: I mean the amphitheatre and the edifice called

Maison Carree.——The former of these is counted the finest monument of the kind now extant; and was built in the reign of Antoninus Pius, who contributed a large sum of money towards its erection. It is of an oval figure, one thousand and eighty feet in circumference, capacious enough to hold twenty thousand spectators. The architecture is of the Tuscan order, sixty feet high, composed of two open galleries, built one over another, consisting each of threescore arcades. The entrance into the arena was by four great gates, with porticos; and the seats, of which there were thirty, rising one above another, consisted of great blocks of stone, many of which still remain. Over the north gate appear two bulls, in *alto relievo*, extremely well executed; emblems which, according to the Romans, signified that the amphitheatre was erected at the expence of the people. There are in other parts of it some works in *bas relief*, and heads or busts but indifferently carved. It stands in the lower part of the town and strikes the spectator with awe and veneration. The external architecture is almost entire in its whole circuit; but the arena is filled up with houses.—This amphitheatre was fortified as a citadel by the Visigoths, in the beginning of the fifth century. They raised within it a castle two towers of which are still extant; and they surrounded it with a broad and deep fossee, which was filled up in the thirteenth century. In all the subsequent wars to which this city was exposed, it served as the last resort of the citizens, and sustained a great number of successive attacks; so that its preservation is almost miraculous. It is likely, however, to suffer much more from the Gothic avarice of its own citizens, some of whom are mutilating it every day, for the sake of the stones, which they employ in their own private buildings. It is surprizing that the King's authority has not been exerted to put an end to such sacriligious violations.

If the Amphitheatre strikes you with an idea of greatness, the *Maison Carree* enchants you with the most exquisite beauties of architecture and sculpture. This is an edifice supposed formerly to have been erected by Adrian, who actually built a basilica in this city, though no vestiges of it remain: but the following inscription, which was discovered on the front of it, plainly proves that it was built by the inhabitants of Nismes, in honour of Caius and Lucius Cæsar, the grandchildren of Augustus, by his daughter Julia, the wife of Agrippa.

C. CAESARI. AVGVSTI. F. COS.
L. CAESARI. AVGVSTI. F. COS.
DESIGNATO.
PRINCIPIBVS JVVENTVTIS.

This beautiful edifice, which stands upon a pediment six feet high, is eighty-two feet long, thirty-five broad, and thirty-seven high, without reckoning the pediment. The body of it is adorned with twenty columns engaged in the wall, and the peri-style, which is open, with ten detached pillars that support the entablature. They are all of the Corinthian order, fluted and embellished with capitals of the most exquisite sculpture; the frize and cornice are much admired, and the foliage is esteemed inimitable. The proportions of the building are so happily united, as to give it an air of majesty and grandeur, which the most indifferent spectator cannot behold without emotion. A man needs not be a connoisseur in architecture to enjoy these beauties. They are indeed so exquisite that you may return to them every day with a fresh appetite, for seven years together. What renders them the more curious, they are still entire, and very little affected, either by the ravages of time or the havoc of war. Cardinal Alberon declared, that it was a jewel that deserved a cover of gold to preserve it from external injuries. An Italian painter, ceiving a part of the roof repaired by modern French masonry, tore his hair, and exclaimed in a rage, "Zounds! what "do I see? Harlequin's hat on the head "of Augustus!"

Without all doubt it is ravishingly beautiful. The whole world cannot parallel it, and I am astonished to see it standing entire, like the effects of inchantment, after such a succession of ages, every one more barbarous than another. The history of the antiquities of Nismes takes notice of a grotesque statue, representing two female bodies and legs, united under the head of an old man; but as it does not inform us where it is kept, I did not see it.

The whole country of Languedoc is shaded with olive trees, the fruit of which begins to ripen, and appears as black as sloes; those they pickle are pulled green, and steeped for some time in a lye made of quick-lime or wood-ashes, which extracts the bitter taste, and makes the fruit tender. Without this preparation it is not eatable. Under the olive and fig trees, they plant corn and vines, so that there is not an inch of ground unlaboured: but there are no open fields, meadows, or cattle to be seen. The ground is overloaded, and the produce of it crowded to such a degree, as to have a bad effect upon the eye, impressing the traveller with the ideas of indigence and rapacity. The heat in summer is so excessive, that cattle would find no green forage, every blade of grass being parched up and destroyed. The weather was extremely hot when we entered Montpellier, and put up at the *Cheval Blanc*, counted the best *auberge* in the place, though in fact it is a most wretched hovel, the habitation of darkness, dirt, and imposition. Here I was obliged to pay four livres a meal for every person in my family, and two livres at night for every bed, though all in the same room. One would imagine that the further we advance to the southward the living is the dearer, though in fact every article of housekeeping is cheaper in Languedoc than many other provinces of France. This imposition is owing to the concourse of English who come hither, and, like simple birds of passage, allow themselves to be plucked by the people of the country, who know their weak side, and make their attacks accordingly. They affect to believe, that all the travellers of our country are, grand seigneurs, immensely rich and incredibly generous; and we are silly enough to encourage this opinion, by submitting quietly to the most ridiculous extortion, as well as by committing all of the most absurd extravagance. The folly of the English, together with a con

LETTER X.

course of people from different quarters, who come hither for the re-establishment of their health, has rendered Montpellier one of the dearest places in the South of France. The city, which is but small, stands upon a rising ground fronting the Mediterranean, which is about three leagues to the southward. on the other side is an agreeable plain, extending about the same distance towards the mountains of the Cevennes. The town is reckoned well built, and what the French call *bien percee*, yet the streets are in general narrow, and the houses dark. The air is counted salutary in catarrhous consumptions, from its dryness and elasticity; but too sharp in cases of pulmonary imposthumes.

It was at Montpellier that we saw for the first time any signs of that gaiety and mirth for which the people of this country are celebrated. In all other places through which we passed since our departure from Lyons, we saw nothing but marks of poverty and chagrin. We entered Montpellier on a Sunday, when the people were all dressed in their best apparel. The streets were crouded; and a great number of the better sort of both sexes sat upon stone seats at their doors, conversing with great mirth and familiarity. These conversations lasted the greatest part of the night; and many of them were improved with music both vocal and instrumental. Next day we were visited by the English residing in the place, who always pay this mark of respect to new comers. They consist of four or five families, among whom I could pass the winter very agreeably, if the state of my health and other reasons did not call me away.

Mr L—— had arrived two days before me troubled with the same asthmatic disorder under which I have laboured so long. He told me he had been in quest of me ever since he left England. Upon comparing notes, I found he had stopped at the door of a country inn in Picardy, and drank a glass of wine and water, while I was at dinner up stairs; nay, he had even spoke to my servant, and asked who was his master, and the man, not knowing him, replied, he was a gentleman from Chelsea. He had walked by the door of the house where I lodged at Paris, twenty times, while I was in that city; and the very day before he arrived at Montpellier, he had passed our coach on the road.

The garrison of this city consists of two battalions, one of which is the Irish regiment of Berwick, commanded by Lieutenant-colonel Tents, a gentleman with whom we contracted an acquaintance at

LETTER X.

Boulogne. He treats us with great politeness, and indeed does every thing in his power to make the place agreeable to us. The duke of Fitz-James, the Governor, is expected here in a little time. We have already a tolerable concert twice a-week; there will be a comedy in the winter, and the states of Provence assemble in January; so that Montpellier will be extremely gay and brilliant. These very circumstances would determine me to leave it. I have not health to enjoy these pleasures I cannot bear a crowd of company, such as pours in upon us unexpectedly at all hours; and I foresee that in staying at Montpellier I should be led into an expence which I can ill afford. I have therefore forwarded the letter I received from general P———n, to Mr B———d, our Consul at Nice, signifying my intention of going thither, and explaining the kind of accommodation I would chuse to have at that place.

The day after our arrival, I procured tolerable lodgings in the High Street, for which I pay fifty sols, something more than two shillings per day; and I am furnished with two meals a day by a *traiteur* for ten livres: but he finds neither the wine nor the desert; and indeed we are but indifferently served. Those families who reside here find their account in keeping house. Every traveller who comes to this or any other town in France with a design to stay longer than a day or two, ought to write beforehand to his correspondent to procure furnished lodgings, to which he may be driven immediately, without being under the necessity of lying in an execrable inn; for all the inns of this country are execrable.

My baggage is not yet arrived by the canal of Languedoc; but that gives me no disturbance, as it is consigned to the care of Mr Ray, an English merchant and banker of this place; a gentleman of great probity and worth, from whom I have received repeated marks of uncommon friendship and hospitality.

The next time you hear of me will be from Nice mean-while I remain always,

Dear Sir,

Your affectionate humble servant.

LETTER XI.

Montpellier, November 14

DEAR DOCTOR,

I Flattered myself with the hope of much amusement during my short stay

LETTER XI.

Montpellier.—The University, the Botanical Garden, the state of physic in this part of the world, and the information I received of a curious collection of manuscripts, among which I hoped to find something for our friend Dr H———r; all these particulars promised a rich fund of entertainment, which, however, I cannot enjoy.

A few days after my arrival, it began to rain with a southerly wind, and continued without ceasing the best part of a week, leaving the air so loaded with vapours, that there was no walking after sun-set, without being wetted by the dew almost to the skin. I have always found a cold and damp atmosphere the most unfavourable of any to my constitution. My asthmatical disorder, which had not given me much disturbance since I left Boulogne, became now very troublesome, attended with fever, cough, spitting, and lowness of spirits; and I wasted visibly every day. I was favoured with the advice of Dr Fitz-Maurice, a very worthy sensible physician settled in this place; but I had the curiosity to know the opinion of the celebrated professor F———, who is the Boerhaave of Montpellier. The account I had of his private character, and personal deportment, from some English people to whom he was well known, left me no desire to converse with him: but I resolved to consult with him on paper. This great lanthorn of medicine is become very rich and very insolent; and in proportion as his wealth increases, he is said to grow the more rapacious. He piques himself upon being very slovenly, very blunt and unmannerly; and perhaps to these qualifications he owes his reputation, rather than to any superior skill in medicine. I have known them succeed in our own country, and seen a doctor's parts estimated by his brutality and presumption.

F—— is in his person and address not unlike our old acquaintance Dr Sm——ie, he stoops much, dodges along, and affects to speak the *Patois*, which is a corruption of the old *Provencial* tongue, spoken by the vulgar in Languedoc and Provence. Notwithstanding his great age and great wealth, he will still scramble up two pair of stairs for a fee of six livres; and without a fee he will give his advice to no person whatsoever. He is said to have great practice in the venereal branch, and to be frequented by persons of both sexes infected with this distemper, not only from every part of France, but also from Spain, Italy, Germany, and England. I need say nothing of the Montpellier method of cure, which is well known at London; but I have some reason to think the great

LETTER XI. 155

professor F—— has, like the famous Mrs Mapp the bone-setter, cured many patients that were never diseased.

Be that as it may, I sent my *valet de place*, who was his townsman and acquaintance, to his house, with the following case, and a loui'dore.

Annum ætatis, post quadragesimum, tertium. Temperamentum humidum, crassum, pituita repletum, catarrhis sæpissime profligatum. Catarrhus, febre, anxietate et dyspnœa, nunquam non comitatus. Irritatio membranæ pituitariæ trachæalis, tussim initio aridam, siliquosam, deinde vero excreationem copiosam excitat: sputum albumini ovi simillimum.

Accedente febre, urina pallida, limpida, ad ἀρχὴν flagrante, colorem rubrum, subflavum induit: coctione peracta, sedimentum lateritium deponit.

Appetitus raro deest. digestio segnior sed secura, non autem sine. Ructu perfecta. Alvus plerumque stipata · excretio intestinalis, minima, ratione ingestorum habita. Pulsus frequens, vacillans, exilis, quandoquidem etiam intermittens.

Febre una extincta, non deficit altera. Aliaque et eadem statim nascitur. Aer paulo rigidior, vel humidior, vestimentum inusitatum indutum; exercitatio paululum nimia, ambulatio, equitatio, in quovis vehiculo jactatio; hæc omnia novos motus suscitant.

Systema nervosum maxime irritabile, organos patitur. Ostiola in cute hiantia, materiei perspirabili, exitum præbentia, clauduntur. Materies obstructa cumulatur; sanguine aliisque humoribus circumagitur fit plethora. Natura opprimi nolens excessus hujus expulsionem conatur. Febris nova accenditur. Pars oneris, in membranam trachealem laxatam ac debilitatam transfertur. Glandulæ pituitariæ turgentes bronchia comprimunt. Liberum aeri transitum negatur. hinc respiratio difficilis. Hac vero translatione febris minuitur: interdiu remittitur. Dyspnæa autem aliaque symptomata vere hypochondriaca, recedere nolunt. Vespere febris exacerbatur. Calor, inquietudo, anxietas et asthma, per noctem grassantur. Ita quotidie res agitur, donec. Vis vitæ paulatim crisim efficit. Seminis jactura, sive in somnis effusi, seu in gremio veneris ejaculati, inter causas horum malorum nec non numeretur.

Quibusdam abhinc annis, exercitationibus juvenilibus subito renatis, in vitam sedentariam lapsum. Animo in studia severiori converso, fibræ gradatim laxabantur. Inter legendum et scribendum inclinato corpore in pectus malum ruebat. Morbo ingruenti affectio scorbutica auxilium tulit. Invasio prima nimium aspernata. Venientibus hostibus non occursum. Cunctando res non restituta. Remidia convenientia stomachus perhorruit,

LETTER XI.

bat. Gravescente dyspnœa phlebotomia frustra tentata. Sanguinis missione vis vitæ diminuta: fiebat pulsus debilior, respiratio difficilior. In pejus ruunt omnia. Febris anomala in febriculam continuam mutata. Dyspnœa confirmata. Fibrarum compages soluta. Valetudo penitus eversa.

His agitatus furiis, æger ad mare provolat: in fluctus se precipitem dat: periculum factum spem non fefellit: decies iteratum, felix faustumque evasit. Elater novus fibris conciliatur. Febricula fugatur. Acris dyspnœa solvitur. Beneficium dextra ripa partum, sinistra perditum. Superficie corporis, æquæ marinæ frigore et pondere compressa et contracta interstitia fibrorum occluduntur: particulis incrementi novis partes obrasas refluentibus, locus non datur. Nutritio corporis, via pristina clausa, qua data porta ruit: in membranam pulmonum munus firmatam facile fertur, et glandulis per sputum ejicitur.

Hieme pluviosa regnante dolores renovantur; tametsi tempore sereno equitatio profuit. Aestate morbus vix vulsum progrediebatur. Autumno, valetudine plus declinata, thermis Bathoniensibus solatium haud frustra quæsitum. Aqua ista mire medicata, externe æque ac interne adhibita, malis levamen attulit. Hiems altera, frigida, horrida, diuturna, innocua tamen successit. Vere novo casus atrox diras procellas animo in-

misit: toto corpore, tota mente tumultuatur. Patria relicta, tristitia, sollicitudo, indignatio, et sævissima recordatio sequuntur. Inimici priores furore inveterato revertuntur. Redit febris hectica: rediit asthma cum anxietate, tusse et dolore lateris lancinanti.

Desperatis denique rebus, iterum ad mare, veluti ad anceps remedium, recurritur. Balneum hoc semper benignum. Dolor statim avolat. Tertio die febris retrocessit. Immersio quotidiana antemeridiana, ad vices quinquaginta repetita, symptomata graviora subjugavit.—Manet vero tabes pituitaria: manet temperamentum in catarrhos proclive. Corpus macrescit. Vires delabantur.

The professor's eyes sparkled at sight of the fee; and he desired the servant to call next morning for his opinion of the case, which accordingly I received in these words:

" On voit par cette relation que monsieur le consultant dont on n'a pas jugé a propos de dire l'age, mais qui nous paroit etre adulte et d'un age passablement avancé, a ete sujet cy devant a des rhumes fréquens accompagnés de fievre; on ne detaille point (aucune epoque,) on parle dans la relation d'asthme auquel il a ete sujet, de scorbut ou affection scorbutique dont on ne dit pas les symptomes. On nous fait scavoir qu'il s'est bien trouve de l'immersion dans l'eau de la mer, et des eaux de Bath.

" On dit a present qu'il a une fievre

LETTER XI.

pituataire, sans dire depuis combien de temps Qu'il lui reste toujours son temperament enclin aux catharres. Qe le corps maigrit, et que les forces se perdent. On ne dit point si'l y a des exacerbations dans cette fievre ou non, si le malade a appetit ou non, s'il tousse ou non, s'il crache ou non: en un mot on n'entre dans aucun detail sur ces objets, sur quoi le conseil soussigné estime que monsieur le consultant est en fievre lente, et que vraisemblable le poumon souffre de quelque tuberçules qui peut-etre sont en fonte, ce que nous aurions determinée si dans la relation on avoit marqué les qualites de crachats.

" La cause fonchere de cette maladie doit etre imputee a une lymphe epaisse et acrimonieuse, qui donne occasion a des tubercules au pomon, qui etant mis en fonte, fournissent au sang des particules acres et le rendent tout acrimonieux.

" Les vues que l'on doit avoir dans ce cas sont de procurer des bonnes digestions (quoique dans la relation on ne dit pas un mot sur les digestions,) de jetter un douce detrempe dans la masse du sang, d'en chasser l'acrimonie et de l'adoucir, de diviser doit doucement la lymphe, et de deterger le poumon, lui procurant meme du calme suppose que la toux l'inquiete, quoique cependant on ne dit pas un mot sur la toux dans la relation. C'est pourquoi on le pur-

LETTER IX.

gera avec 3 onces de manne, diffoutes dans un verre de decoction de 3 dragmes de polypode de chefne, on paffera enfuite a des bouillons qui feront faits avec un petit poulet, la chair, le fang, le cœur et le foye d'une tortue de grandeur mediocre, c'eft adire du poid de 8 a 12 onces avec fa coquille, une poignee de chicoree amere de jardin, et une pincee de feuilles de lierre terreftre vertes ou feches. Ayant pris ces bouillons 15 matins on fe purgera comme auparavant, pour en venir a des bouillons qui feront faits avec la moitie d'un mou de veau, une poignee de pimprenelle de jardin, et une dragme de racine d'angelique concaffee.

Ayant pris ces bouillons 15 matins, on fe purgera comme auparavant pour en venir au lait d'aneffe que l'on pendra le matin a jeun, a la dofe de 12 a 16 onces y ajoutant un cuilleree de fucre rape, on prendra ce lait le matin a jeun obfervant de prendre pendant fon ufage de deux jours l'un un moment avant le lait un bolus fait avec 15 grains de craye de Briançon en poudre fine, 20 grains de coral prepare, 8 grains d'antihectique de poterius, et ce qu'il faut de fyrop de lierre terreftre, mais les jour ou on ne prendra pas le bolus on prendra un moment avant le lait 3 ou 4 gouttes de bon baume de Canada detrempees das un demi cuilleree

LETTER XI.

de syrop de lierre terrestre. Si le corps maigrit de plus en plus, je suis d'avis que pendant l'usage du lait d'anesse on soupe tous les sois avec une soupe au lait de vache.

" On continuera l'usage du lait d'anesse tant, que le malade pourra le supporter, ne le purgeant que par necessite, et toujours avec la medicine ordonnee.

" Au reste, si monsiuer le consultant ne passe pas les nuits bien calmes, il prendra chaque soir a l'heure de sommeil six grains des pilules de cynoglosse, dont il augmentera la dose d'un grain de plus toutes les fois que la dose du jour precedent, n'aura pas ete suffisante pour lui faire passer la nuit bien calme.

" Si les malade touffe il usera soit de jour soit de nuit par petites cuilleries a caffe d'n looch, qui sera fait avec un once de syrop de violat et une dragme de blanc de baleine.

" Si les crachats sont epais et qu'uil crache difficilement, en ce cas il prendra, une ou deux fois le jour, demi dragme de blanc de baleine reduit en poudre avec un peu de sucre candit, qu'il avalera avec une cuillerie d'eau.

" Enfin, il doit observer un bon regime de vivre, c'est pourquoi il sera toujours gras et seulement en soupes, bouilli et roti, il ne mangera pas les herbes des soupes, et on salera peu son pot, il se privera du beuf, cochon, chair noir, oiseaux d'eau, ragouts, fritures, patisseries, alimens sales, epices, vinagres, salades, fruits, cruds, et autres crudites, alimens grossiers, ou de difficille digestion, la boisson sera de l'eau tant soit peu rougee de bon vin au diner seulement, et il ne prendra a soupe, qu'une soupe.

F———,

Delibere a Montpellier
le 11 Novambre.   Prof. sluer en l'université honoraire

Receu vint et quatre livres"

I thought it was a little extraordinary that a learned professor should reply in his mother tongue to a case put in Latin; but I was much more surprised, as you will also be, at reading his answer, from which I was obliged to conclude, either that he did not understand Latin, or that he had not taken the trouble to read my *memoire*. I shall not make any remarks upon the style of his prescription, replete as it is with a disgusting repetition of low expressions: but I could not but, in justice to myself, point out to him the passages in my case which he had overlooked. Accordingly, having marked them with letters, I sent it back, with the following billet.

" Apparement Monsf. F——— n'a pas

donne beaucoup d'attention au memoire de ma fante qua j'ai eu l'honneur de lui prefenter—' Monfieur le confultant (dit ' il) dont on n'a pas jugé a propos de dire ' l'age.'---Mais on voit dans le memoire a No. 1. '*Annum ætatis poft quadragefi-* '*mum tertium.*'

"Mr F—— dit que ' je n'ai pas marqué aucune epoque.' Mais a No. 2. du memoire il trouvera ces mots, '*Quibuf-* '*dam abhinc annis.*' J'ai meme detaillé le progrès de la maladie pour trois ans confecutifs.

"Monf. F—— obferve, ' On ne dit ' point s'il y a des exacerbations dans cet- ' te fievre ou non.' Qu'il regarde la lettre B, il verra, '*Vefpere febris exacerba-* '*tur. Calor, inquietudo, anxietas et afth-* '*ma per noctem graffantur.*'

"Monf. F—— remarque, ' On ne dit ' point fi le malade a appetit ou non, s'il touffe ou non, s'il crache ou non ; en un ' mot, on n'entre dans aucun detail fur ' ces objets. Mais on voit toutes ces circonftances detaillees dans le memoire a lettre A, '*Irritatio membranæ trachealis* tuffim, initio aridam, filiquofam, deinde vero excreationem copiofam excitat. Sputum albumini ovi fimillimum. Appetitus raro deeft. Digeftio fegnior fed fecura.'

"Monf. F—— obferve encore, ' qu'on ne dit pas un mot fur la toux dans la re-

' lation.' Mas j'ai dit encore a No. 3. de memoire, ' *Redit febris hectica, re-* ' *dit asthma cum anxietate,* tusse *et do-* ' *lore lateris lancinante.*'

" Au reste, je ne puis pas me persuader qu'il y ait des tubercules au poumon, parce que j'ai ne jamais crache de pus, ni autre chose que de la pituite qui a beaucoup de resemblance au blanc des oeufs. *Sputum albumini ovi simillimum.* Il me paroit donc que ma maladie doit son origine a la suspension de l'exercice du corps, au grand attachement d'esprit, et a une vie sedentaire qui a relache le sisteme fibreux; et qu'a present en peut l'appeller *tabes pituitaria,* non *tabes purulenta.* J'espere que Monsf. F—— aura la bonte de faire revision du memoire, et de m'en dire encore son sentiment."

Considering the nature of the case, you see I could not treat him more civilly. I desired the servant to ask when he should return for an answer, and whether he expected another fee. He desired him to come next morning; and, as the fellow assured me, gave him to understand, that whatever monsieur might send, should be for his (the servant's) advantage. In all probability he did not expect another gratification, to which, indeed, he had no title. Monsf. F—— was undoubtedly much mortified to find himself detected in such

LETTER XI.

flagrant instances of unjustifiable negligence; and, like all other persons in the same ungracious dilemma, instead of justifying himself by reason or argument, had recourse to recrimination. In the paper which he sent me next day, he insisted in general that he had carefully perused the case, (which you will perceive was a self-evident untruth;) he said the theory it contained was idle; that he was sure it could not be written by a physician, that, with respect to the disorder, he was still of the same opinion, and adhered to his former prescription; but if I had any doubts I might come to his house, and he would resolve them.

I wrapt up twelve livres in the following note, and sent it to his house.

"C'est ne pas sans raison que monsieur F—— jouit d'un si grande reputation. Je n'ai plus de doutes, graces a Dieu et a monsieur F——e."

To this I received for answer, "Monsieur n'a plus de doubtes; j'en suis charmé. Receu douze livres. F——, &c.

Instead of keeping his promise to the valet, he put the money in his pocket; and the fellow returned in a rage, exclaiming that he was *un gross cheval de mousse*.

I shall make no other comment upon the medicines and the regimen which this great doctor prescribed, but that he certainly mistook the case: that upon the supposition I actually laboured under a purulent discharge from the lungs, his remedies favour strongly of the old woman; and that there is a total blank with respect to the article of exercise, which you know is so essential in all pulmonary disorders. But after having perused my remarks upon his first prescription, he could not possibly suppose that I had tubercules, and was spitting up pus; therefore his persisting in recommending the same medicines he had prescribed on that supposition, was a flagrant absurdity.---If, for example, there was no *vomica* in the lungs, and the business was to attentuate the lymph, what could be more preposterous than to advise the chalk of Briancon, coral, anti hecticum poterii, and the balm of Canada! As for the turtle-soupe, it is a good restorative and balsamic; but, I apprehend, will tend to thicken rather than attentuate the phlegm. He mentions not a syllable of the air, though it is universally allowed that the climate of Montpellier is pernicious to ulcerated lungs. And here I cannot help recounting a small adventure which our doctor had with a son of Mr O———d, merchant in the city of London. I had it from Mrs St---e who was on the spot. The young gentleman be ing confumptive, confulted Mr F——, who continued vifiting and prefcribing for him a whole month. At length perceiving that he grew daily worfe, "Doctor, (faid he,) I take your prefcriptions punctually; but, inftead of being the better for them, I have now not an hour's remiffion from the fever in the four-and-twenty.——I cannot conceive the meaning of it." F——, who perceived he had not long to live, told him the reafon was very plain: the air of Montpellier was too fharp for his lungs, which required a fofter climate. "Then your a fordid villain (cried the young man) for allowing me to ftay here till my conftitution is irretrievable." He fet out immediadely for Tholoufe, and in a few weeks died in the neighbourhood of that city.

I obferve that the phyficians in this country pay no regard to the ftate of the folids in chronical diforders: that exercife and the cold bath are never prefcribed: that they feem to think the fcurvy is entirely an Englifh difeafe; and that, in all appearance, they often confound the fymptoms of it with thofe of the venereal diftemper. Perhaps I may be more particular on this fubject in a fubfequent letter. In the mean time, am ever,

Dear Sir,

Yours fincerely.

LETTER XII.

Nice, December 6, 1763.

DEAR SIR,

THE inhabitants of Montpellier are sociable, gay, and good tempered. They have a spirit of commerce, and have erected several considerable manufactures in the neighbourhood of the city. People assemble every day to take the air on the esplanade, where there is a very good walk, just without the gate of the citadel: but, on the other side of the town, there is another still more agreeable, called the *peirou*, from whence there is a prospect of the Mediterranean on one side, and of the Cevennes on the other. Here is a good equestrian statue of Louis XIV. fronting one gate of the city, which is built in form of a triumphal arch, in honour of the same monarch. Immediately under the *peirou* is the physic garden, and near it an arcade just finished for an aqueduct, to convey a stream of water to the upper parts of the city. Perhaps I should have thought this a neat piece of work, if I had not seen the *Pont du Garde*: but after having viewed the Roman arches,

LETTER XII.

could not look upon this but with pity and contempt. It is a wonder how the architect could be so fantastically modern, having such a noble model, as it were, before his eyes.

There are many Protestants at this place as well as at Nismes, and they are no longer molested on the score of religion. They have their conventicles in the country, where they assemble privately for worship. These are well known; and detachments are sent out every Sunday to intercept them; but the officer has always private directions to take another route. Whether this indulgence comes from the wisdom and lenity of the government, or is purchased with money of the commanding officer, I cannot determine: but certain it is, the laws of France punish capitally every Protestant minister convicted of having performed the functions of his ministry in this kingdom; and one was hanged about two years ago in the neighbourhood of Montauban.

The markets in Montpellier are well supplied with fish, poultry, butcher's meat, and game, at reasonable rates. The wine of the country is strong and harsh, and never drank but when mixed with water. Burgundy is dear, and so is the sweet wine of Frontignan, though made in the neighbourhood of Cette. You know it is famous all over Europe, and so are the *liquers*, or drams of various sorts, compounded and distilled at Montpelier. Cette is the sea-port, about four leagues from that city; but the canal of Languedoc comes up within a mile of it; and is indeed a great curiosity. a work in all respects worthy of a Colbert, under whose auspices it was finished. When I find such a general tribute of respect and veneration paid to the memory of that great man, I am astonished to see so few monuments of public utility left by other ministers. One would imagine, that even the desire of praise would prompt a much greater number to exert themselves for the glory and advantage of their country; yet, in my opinion, the French have been ungrateful to Colbert, in the same proportion as they have over-rated the character of his master. Through all France one meets with statues and triumphal arches erected to Louis XIV. in consequence of his victories; by which, likewise, he acquired the title of Louis le Grand. But how were those victories obtained? Not by any personal merit of Louis. It was Colbert who improved his finances, and enabled him to pay his army. It was Louvois that provided all the necessaries of war. It was a Conde, a Turenne, a Luxemburg, a Vendome, who fought his battles; and his first conquests, for which he was deified by the pen of adulation, were obtained almost without bloodshed, over weak, dispirited, divided, and defenseless nations. It was Colbert that improved the marine, instituted manufactures, encouraged commerce, undertook works of public utility, and patronized the arts and sciences. But Lewis (you will say) had the merit of chusing and supporting those ministers and those generals. I answer, no. He found Colbert and Louvois already chosen: he found Conde and Turenne in the very zenith of military reputation. Luxemburg was Conde's pupil; and Vendome a prince of the blood, who at first obtained the command of armies in consequence of his high birth, and happened to turn out a man of genius. The same Louis had the sagacity to revoke the edict of Nantz; to entrust his armies to a Tallord, a Villeroy, and a Marsin. He had the humanity to ravage the country, burn the towns, and massacre the people of the Palatinate. He had the patriotism to impoverish and depopulate his own kingdom, in order to prosecute schemes of the most lawless ambition. He had the consolation to beg a piece from those he had provoked to war by the most outrageous insolence; and he had the glory to espouse Mrs Maintenon in her old age, the widow of the buffoon Scarron. Without all doubt it was from irony he acquired the title *le Grand*.

Having received a favourable answer from Mr B——, the English consul at Nice, and recommended the care of my heavy baggage to Mr Ray, who undertook to send it to sea from Cette to Villefranche, I hired a coach and mules for seven loui'dores, and set out from Montpellier on the 13th of November, the weather being agreeable, though the air was cold and frosty. In other respects there were no signs of winter: the olives were now ripe, and appeared on each side of the road as black as sloes; and the corn was already half a foot high. On the second day of our journey, we passed the Rhone on a bridge of boats at Buccaire, and lay on the other side at Tarascone. Next day we put up at a wretched place called Orgon, where however, we were regaled with an excellent supper; and, among other delicacies, with a dish of green pease. Provence is a pleasant country, well cultivated; but the inns are not so good here as in Languedoc, and few of them are provided with a certain convenience which an English traveller can very ill dispense with. Those you find are generally on the tops of houses, exceedingly nasty; and so much exposed to the weather, that

Valetudinarian cannot use them without hazard of his life. At Nismes in Languedoc, where we found the temple of Cloacina in a most shocking condition, the servant-maid told me her mistress had caused it to be made on purpose for the English travellers; but now she was very sorry for what she had done, as all the French who frequented her house, instead of using the seat, left their offerings on the floor, which she was obliged to have cleared three or four times a day. This is a degree of beastliness which would appear detestable even in the capital of North Britain. On the fourth day of our pilgrimage, we lay in the suburbs of Aix, but did not enter the city, which I had great a curiosity to see. The villanous asthma baulked me of that satisfaction. I was pinched with the cold, and impatient to reach a warmer climate. Our next stage was at a paltry village, where we were poorly entertained. I looked so ill in the morning, that the good woman of the house, who was big with child, took me by the hand at parting, and even shed tears, praying fervently that God would restore me to my health. This was the he only instance of sympathy, compassion, or goodness of heart, that I had met with among the publicans of France. Indeed, at Valencia, our landlady understanding that I was travelling to Montpellier for my health, would have diſſuaded me from going thither; and exhorting me, in particular, to beware of the phyſicians, who were all a pack of aſſaſſins. She adviſed me to eat fricaſſees of chickens, and white meat, and to take a good *bouillon* every morning.

A *bouillon* is an univerſal remedy among the good people of France; inſomuch that they have no idea of any perſon's dying after having ſwallowed *un bon bouillon*. One of the Engliſh gentlemen who were robbed and murdered about thirty years ago between Calais and Boulogne, being brought to the poſt-houſe of Boulogne with ſome ſigns of life, this remedy was immediately adminiſtred. "What ſurpriſes me greatly, (ſaid the poſt-maſter, ſpeaking of this melancholy ſtory to a friend of mine, two years after it happened,) I made an excellent *bouillon*, and poured it down his throat with my own hands, and yet he did not recover." Now in all probability, this *bouillon* it was that ſtopped his breath. When I was a very young man, I remember to have ſeen a perſon ſuffocated by ſuch impertinent officiouſneſs. A young man of uncommon parts and erudition, very well eſteemed at the univerſity of G——ow, was found early one morning in a ſubterranean vault among the ruins of an old archi-episcopal palace, with his throat cut from ear to ear. Being conveyed to a public house in the neighbourhood, he made signs for pen, ink, and paper; and in all probability would have explained the cause of this terrible catastrophe, when an old woman seeing the windpipe, which was cut, sticking out of the wound, and mistaking it for the gullet, by way of giving him a cordial to support his spirits, poured into it, through a small funnel, a glass of burnt brandy, which strangled him in the tenth part of a minute. The gash was so hideous, and formed by so many repeated strokes of a razor, that the surgeons believed he could not possibly be the perpetrator himself; nevertheless, this was certainly the case.

At Brignolles, where we dined, I was obliged to quarrel with the landlady, and threaten to leave her house, before she would indulge us with any sort of flesh-meat. It was meagre-day, and she had made her provision accordingly. She even hinted some dissatisfaction at having heretics in her house: but, as I was not disposed to eat stinking fish, with ragouts of eggs and onions, I insisted upon a leg of mutton, and a brace of fine partridges, which I found in the larder. Next day, when we set out in the morning from Luc, it blew a north-westerly wind so excessively cold and biting, that even a flannel wrapper could not keep me tolerably warm in the coach. Whether the cold had put our coachman in a bad humour, or he had some other cause of resentment against himself, I know not; but we had not gone above a quarter of a mile, when he drove the carriage full against the corner of a garden wall, and broke the axle-tree, so that we were obliged to return to the inn on foot, and wait a whole day, until a new piece could be made and adjusted. The wind that blew, is called *Maestral*, in the Provencial dialect, and indeed is the severest that ever I felt. At this inn we met with a young French officer who had been a prisoner in England, and spoke our language pretty well. He told me, that such a wind did not blow above twice or three times in a winter, and was never of long continuance: that, in general, the weather was very mild and agreeable during the winter months: that living was very cheap in this part of Provence, which afforded great plenty of game. Here, too, I found a young Irish recollet, in his way from Rome to his own country. He complained that he was almost starved by the inhospitable disposition of the French people: and that the regular clergy, in particular, had treated him with the most cruel disdain. I relieved his necessities, and gave him a letter to a gentleman of his own country at Montpellier.

When I rose in the morning, and opened a window that looked into the garden, I thought myself either in a dream, or bewitched. All the trees were cloathed with snow, and all the country covered at least a foot thick. "This cannot be the south " of France, (said I to myself,) it must " be the Highlands of Scotland!" At a wretched town called Muy, where we dined, I had a warm dispute with our landlord, which, however, did not terminate to my satisfaction. I sent on my mules before, to the next stage, resolving to take post horses, and bespoke them accordingly of the aubergiste, who was, at the same time, inn-keeper and post-master. We were ushered into the common eating room, and had a very indifferent dinner; after which I sent a louis'dore to be changed, in order to pay the reckoning. The landlord, instead of giving the full change, deducted three livres a head for dinner, and sent in the rest of the money by my servant. Provoked more at his ill manners than at his extortion, I ferreted him out of a bedchamber where he had concealed himself, and obliged him to restore the full change, from which I paid him at the rate of two livres a head. He refused to take the money, which I threw down on the table;

and the horses being ready, stepped into the coach, ordering the postilions to drive on. Here I had certainly reckoned without my host. The fellows declared they would not budge, until I should pay their master; and as I threatened them with manual chastisement, they alighted and disappeared in a twinkling. I was now so incensed, that though I could hardly breathe, though the afternoon was far advanced, and the street covered with wet snow, I walked to the consul of the town, and made my complaint in form. This magistrate, who seemed to be a taylor, accompanied me to the inn, where by this time the whole town was assembled, and endeavoured to compromise the affair. I said, as he was the magistrate, I would stand to his award. He answered, " that he would not pre- " sume to determine what I was to pay." I have already paid him a reasonable price for his dinner, (said I,) and now I demand post-horses, according to the king's ordonnance. The aubergiste said the horses were ready, but the guides were run away; and he could not find others to go in their place. I argued with great vehemence, offering to leave a loui'dore for the poor of the parish, provided the consul would oblige the rascal to do his duty. The consul shrugged up his shoulders, and declared was not in his power. This was a lie, but

I perceived he had no mind to disoblige the publican. If the mules had not been sent away, I should certainly have not only paid what I thought proper, but corrected the landlord into the bargain, for his insolence and extortion: but now I was entirely at his mercy, and as the consul continued to exhort me, in very humble terms, to comply with his demands, I thought proper to aquiesce. Then the postilions immediately appeared: the crowd seemed to exult in the triumph of the aubergiste; and I was obliged to travel in the night, in very severe weather, after all the fatigue and mortification I had undergone.

We lay at Frejus, which was the *Forum Julianum* of the Antients, and still boasts of some remains of antiquity; particularly the ruins of an amphitheatre, and an aqueduct. The first we passed in the dark, and next morning the weather was so cold that I could not walk abroad to see it. The town is at present very inconsiderable, and indeed in a ruinous condition. Nevertheless we were very well lodged at the post-house, and treated with more politeness than we had met with in any other part of France.

As we had a very high mountain to ascend in the morning, I ordered the mules on before to the next post, and hired six mules for the coach. At the east end of

Frejus we saw, close to the road on our left hand, the arcades of the antient aqueduct, and the ruins of some Roman edifices, which seemed to have been temples. There was nothing striking in the architecture of the aqueduct. The arches are small and low, without either grace or ornament, and seem to have been calculated for mere utility.

The mountain of Esterelles, which is eight miles over, was formerly frequented by a gang of desperate banditti, who are now happily exterminated: the road is very good, but in some places very steep, and bordered by precipices. The mountain is covered with pines, and the *laurus cerasus*, the fruit of which being now ripe, made a most romantic appearance through the snow that lay upon the branches. The cherries were so large that I at first mistook them for dwarf oranges. I think they are counted poisonous in England, but here the people eat them without hesitation. In the middle of the mountain is the post-house, where we dined in a room so cold, that the bare remembrance of it makes my teeth chatter. After dinner I chanced to look into another chamber that fronted the south, where the sun shone; and opening a window, perceived, within a yard of my hand, a large tree loaded with oranges, many of which were ripe. You may judge what

LETTER XII.

my astonishment was to find Winter in all his rigour reigning on one side of the house, and Summer in all her glory on the other. Certain it is, the middle of this mountain seemed to be the boundary of the cold weather. As we proceeded slowly in the afternoon, we were quite enchanted This side of the hill is a natural plantation of the most agreeable ever-greens, pines, firs, laurel, cypress, sweet myrtle, tamarisk, box, and juniper, interspersed with sweet marjoram, lavender, thyme, wild thyme, and sage. On the right-hand the ground shoots up into agreeable cones, between which you have delightful vistas of the Mediterranean, which washes the foot of the rock; and between two divisions of the mountains, there is a bottom watered by a charming stream, which greatly adds to the rural beauties of the scene.

This night we passed at Cannes, a little fishing town, agreeably situated on the beach of the sea, and in the same place lodged Monsieur Nadeau d'Etruail, the unfortunate French governor of Guadaloupe, condemned to be imprisoned for life in one of the isles Muaguerite, which lye within a mile of this coast

Next day we journeyed by the way of Antibes, a small maritime town, tolerably well fortified; and passing the little river Loup, over a stone-bridge, arrived about noon at the Village of St Laurent, the extremity of France, where we paſſed the Var, after our baggage had undergone examination. From Cannes to this Village the road lyes along the ſeaſide; and ſure nothing can be more delightful. Though in the morning there was a froſt upon the ground, the ſun was as warm as it is in May in England. The ſea was quite ſmooth, and the beach formed of white poliſhed pebbles; on the left hand the country was covered with green olives, and the ſide of the road planted with large trees of ſweet myrtle growing wild like the hawthorns in England. From Antibes we had the firſt view of Nice, lying on the oppoſite ſide of the bay, and making a very agreeable appearance. The author of the Grand Tour ſays, that from Antibes to Nice the roads are very bad, through rugged mountains bordered with precipices on the left, and by the ſea to the right; whereas, in fact, there is neither precipice nor mountain near it.

The Var, which divides the county of Nice from Provence, is no other than a torrent fed chiefly by the ſnow that melts on the maritime Alps, from which it takes its origin. In the ſummer it is ſwelled to a dangerous height, and this is alſo the caſe after heavy rains; but at preſent the middle of it is quite dry, and the water divided into two or three narrow streams, which however are both deep and rapid. This river has been absurdly enough by some supposed the Rubicon, in all probability from the description of that river in the Pharsalia of Lucan, who makes it the boundary betwixt Gaul and Italy——

————————et Gallica certus
Limes ab Ausoniis disterminat arva colonis;

whereas, in fact, the Rubicon, now called Pisatello, runs between Ravenna and Rimini.——But to return to the Var. At the village of St Laurent, famous for its Muscadine wines, there is a set of guides always in attendance to conduct you in your passage over the river. Six of those fellows, tucked up above the middle, with long poles in their hands, took charge of our coach, and by many windings guided it safe to the opposite shore. Indeed there was no occasion for any: but it is a sort of a perquisite, and I did not chuse to run any risque, how small soever it might be, for the sake of saving half a crown, with which they were satisfied. If you do not gratify the searchers at St Laurent with the same sum, they will rummage your trunks, and turn all your clothes topsy turvy. And here, once for all, I would advise every traveller who consults his own ease and convenience, to be liberal of his money to all that sort of people; and even to wink at the imposition of aubergistes on the road, unless it be very flagrant. So sure as you enter into disputes with them, you will be put to a great deal of trouble, and fret yourself to no manner of purpose. I have travelled with œconomists in England, who declared they would rather give away a crown than allow themselves to be cheated of a farthing. This is a good maxim, but requires a great share of resolution and self-denial to put in practice in one excursion. My fellow-traveller was in a passion, and of consequence very bad company from one end of the journey to the other. He was incessantly scolding either at landlords, landladies, waiters, hostlers, or postilions. We had bad horses, and bad chaises; set out from every stage with the curses of the people; and at this expence I saved about ten shillings in a journey of a hundred and fifty miles. For such a paultry consideration, he was contented to be miserable himself, and to make every other person unhappy with whom he had any concern. When I came last from Bath it rained so hard, that the postilion who drove the chaise was wet to the skin before we had gone a couple of miles. When we arrived at the Devizes,

LETTER XII.

I gave him two shillings instead of one, out of pure compassion. The consequence of this liberality was, that in the next stage we seemed rather to fly than to travel upon solid ground. I continued my bounty to the second driver, and indeed through the whole journey, and found myself accommodated in a very different manner from what I had experienced before. I had elegant chaises, with excellent horses; and the postilions of their own accord used such diligence, that although the roads were broken by the rain, I travelled at the rate of twelve miles an hour; and my extraordinary expence from Bath to London, amounted precisely to six shillings.

The river Var falls into the Mediterranean a little below St Laurent, about four miles to the westward of Nice. Within the memory of persons now living, there have been three wooden bridges thrown over it, and as often destroyed in consequence of the jealousy subsisting between the kings of France and Sardinia; this river being the boundary of their dominions on the side of Provence. However, this is a consideration that ought not to interfere with the other advantages that would accrue to both kingdoms from such a convenience. If there was a bridge over the Var, and a post-road made from

Nice to Genoa, I am very confident that all those strangers who now pass the Alps in their way to and from Italy, would chuse this road, as infinitely more safe, commodious, and agreeable. This would also be the case with all those who hire felucas from Marseilles or Antibes, and expose themselves to the dangers and inconveniencies of travelling by sea in an open boat.

In the afternoon we arrived at Nice, where we found Mr M———e, the English gentleman whom I had seen at Boulogne, and advised to come hither. He had followed my advice, and reached Nice about a month before my arrival, with his lady, child, and an old gouvernante. He had travelled with his own post-chaise and horses, and is now lodged just without one of the gates of the city, in the house of the Count de V———a, for which he pays five louis' dores a month. I could hire one much better in the neighbourhood of London for the same money. Unless you will submit to this extortion, and hire a whole house for a length of time, you will find no ready-furnished lodgings at Nice. After having flewed a week in a paltry inn, I have taken a ground-floor for ten months at the rate of four hundred livres a year, that is precisely twenty pounds sterling, for the Piedmontese livre is exactly an Eng'sh shilling. The apartments are large, lofty, and commodious enough, with two small gardens, in which there is plenty of sallad, and a great number of oranges and lemons: but as it required some time to provide furniture, our consul Mr B——d, one of the best-natured and most friendly men in the world, has lent me his lodgings, which are charmingly situated by the sea-side, and open upon a terrace, that runs parallel to the beach, forming part of the town wall. Mr B——d himself lives at Villa Franca, which is divided from Nice by a single mountain, on the top of which there is a small fort, called *the castle of Montalban*. Immediately after our arrival we were visited by one Mr de Martines, a most agreeable young fellow, a lieutenant in the Swifs regiment, which is here in garrison. He is a Protestant, extremely fond of our nation, and understands our language tolerably well. He was particularly recommended to our acquaintance by general P—— and his lady; we are happy in his conversation; find him wonderfully obliging, and extremely serviceable on many occasions. We have likewise made acquaintance with some other individuals, particularly with M. St Pierre, junior, who is a considerable merchant, and consul for Naples. He is a well-bred, sensible young man, speaks

LETTER XII.

English, is an excellent performer on the lute and mandolin, and has a pretty collection of books. In a word, I hope we shall pass the winter agreeably enough, especially if Mr M——e should hold out; but I am afraid he is too far gone in a consumption to recover. He spent the last winter at Nismes, and consulted F—— at Montpellier. I was impatient to see the prescription, and found it almost verbatim the same he had sent to me; although I am persuaded there is a very essential difference between our disorders. Mr M——e has been long afflicted with violent spasms, colliquative sweats, prostration of appetite, and a disorder in his bowels. He is likewise jaundized all over, and I am confident his liver is unsound. He tried the tortoise soup, which he said in a fortnight stuffed him up with phlegm. This gentleman has got a smattering of physic, and I am afraid tampers with his own constitution, by means of Brooke's Practice of Physic, and some dispensatories, which he is continually poring over. I beg pardon for this tedious epistle, and am,

Very sincerely, dear Sir,

Your affectionate

Humble servant,

LETTER XIII.

Nice, January 15, 1764.

DEAR SIR,

I AM at last settled at Nice, and have leisure to give you some account of this very remarkable place. The county of Nice extends about fourscore miles in length, and in some places it is thirty miles broad. It contains several small towns, and a great number of villages; all of which, this capital excepted, are situated among mountains, the most extensive plain of the whole country being this where I now am, in the neighbourhood of Nice. The length of it does not exceed two miles, nor is the breadth of it, in any part, above one. It is bounded by the Mediterranean on the south. From the sea-shore, the maritime Alps begin with hills of a gentle ascent, rising into mountains that form a sweep or amphitheatre ending at Montalban, which over-hangs the Town of Villa Franca. On the west side of this mountain, and in the eastern extremity of the amphitheatre, stands the city of Nice, wedged in between a steep rock and the little river

Paglion, which descends from the mountains, and washing the town-walls on the west side, falls into the sea, after having filled some canals for the use of the inhabitants. There is a stone-bridge of three arches over it, by which those who come from Provence enter the city. The channel of it is very broad, but generally dry in many places; the water (as in the Var) dividing itself into several small streams. The Paglion being fed by melted snow and rain in the mountains, is quite dry in summer; but it is sometimes swelled by sudden rains to a very formidable torrent. This was the case in the year 1744, when the French and Spanish armies attacked eighteen Piedmontese battalions, which were posted on the side of Montalban. The assailants were repulsed with the loss of four thousand men, some hundreds of whom perished in repassing the Paglion, which had swelled to a surprising degree during the battle, in consequence of a heavy continued rain. This rain was of great service to the Piedmontese, as it prevented one half of the enemy from passing the river to sustain the other. Five hundred were taken prisoners: but the Piedmontese, forseeing they should be surrounded next day by the French, who had penetrated behind them, by a pass in the mountains, retired in the night. Bein received on board the English fleet, which lay at Villa Franca, they were conveyed to Oneglia. In examining the bodies of them that were killed in the battle, the inhabitants of Nice perceived that a great number of the Spanish soldiers were circumcised; a circumstance from which they concluded, that a great many Jews engaged in the service of his Catholic majesty. I am of a different opinion. The Jews are the least of any people that I know addicted to a military life. I rather imagine they were of the Moorish race, who have subsisted in Spain since the expulsion of their brethren; and though they conform externally to the rites of the Catholic religion, still retain in private their attachment to the law of Mahomet.

The city of Nice is built in form of an irregular isosceles triangle, the base of which fronts the sea. On the west side it is surrounded by a wall and rampart; on the east, it is over-hung by a rock, on which we see the ruins of an old castle, which, before the invention of artillery, was counted impregnable. It was taken and dismantled by marechal Catinat, in the time of Victor Amadœus, the father of his Sardinian majesty. It was afterwards finally demolished by the Duke of Berwick, towards the latter end of Queen Anne's war. To repair it would be a very unnecessary expence, as it is commanded by Montalban and several other eminences.

The town of Nice is altogether indefensible, and therefore without fortifications. There are only two iron guns upon a bastion that fronts the beach; and here the French had formed a considerable battery against the English cruisers, in the war of 1744, when the Mareschal Duke de Belleisle had his head-quarters at Nice. This little town, situated in the bay of Antibes, is almost equidistant from Marseilles, Turin, and Genoa, the first and last being about thirty leagues from hence by sea; and the capital of Piedmont at the same distance to the northward, over the mountains. It lyes exactly opposite to Capo di Ferro, on the coast of Barbary; and the islands of Sardinia and Corsica are laid down about two degrees to the eastward, almost exactly in a line with Genoa. This little town, hardly a mile in circumference, is said to contain twelve thousand inhabitants. The streets are narrow; the houses are built of stone, and the windows in general are fitted with paper instead of glass. This expedient would not answer in a country subject to rain and storms, but here, where there is very little of either, the paper lozenges answer tolerably well. The bourgeois however, begin to have their houses sash ed with glass. Between the town-wall and the sea, the fishermen haul up their boats upon the open beach; but on the other side of the rock, where the castle stood, is the port or harbour of Nice, upon which some money has been expended. It is a small basin, defended to sea-ward by a mole of free-stone, which is much better contrived than executed: for the sea has already made three breaches in it; and in all probability, in another winter, the extremity of it will be carried quite away. It would require the talents of a very skilful architect to lay the foundation of a good mole, on an open beach like this, exposed to the swell of the whole Mediterranean, without any island or rock in the offing, to break the force of the waves. Besides, the shore is bold, and the bottom foul. There are seventeen feet of water in the basin, sufficient to float vessels of one hundred and fifty ton; and this is chiefly supplied by a small stream of very fine water; another great convenience for shipping. On the side of the mole here is a constant guard of soldiers, and a battery of seven cannon, pointing to the sea. On the other side there is a curious manufacture for twisting or reeling silk; a tavern, a coffee-house, and several other buildings, for the convenience of the sea-faring people. Without the harbour is a lazarette, where persons coming from infected places, are obliged to perform quarantine. The harbour has been declared a free-port, and it is generally full of tartanes, polacres, and other small vessels, that come from Sardinia, Ivica, Italy, and Spain, loaded with salt, wine, and other commodities; but here is no trade of any great consequence.

The city of Nice is provided with a senate, which administers justice under the auspices of an avocat-general, sent hither by the king. The internal œconomy of the town is managed by four consuls, one for the noblesse, another for the merchants, a third for the bourgeois, and a fourth for the peasants. These are chosen annually from the town-council. They keep the streets and markets in order, and superintend the public works. There is also an intendant, who takes care of his majesty's revenue. but there is a discretionary power lodged in the person of the commandant, who is always an officer of rank in the service, and has under his immediate command the regiment which is here in garrison. That which is here now is a Swiss battalion, of which the king has five or six in his service. There is likewise a regiment of militia, which is exercised once a year. But of all these particulars I shall speak more fully on another occasion.

LETTER XIII.

When I stand upon the rampart, and look round me, I can scarce help thinking myself inchanted. The small extent of country which I see, is all cultivated like a garden. Indeed the plain presents nothing but gardens, full of green trees, loaded with oranges, lemons, citrons, and bergamots, which make a delightful appearance. If you examine them more nearly, you will find plantations of green peafe ready to gather; all forts of fallading, and pot herbs, in perfection, and plats of rofes, carnations, ranunculas, anemonies, and daffodils, blowing in full glory, with such beauty, vigour, and perfume, as no flower in England ever exhibited.

I must tell you, that presents of carnations are sent from hence, in the winter, to Turin and Paris; nay, sometimes as far as London, by the post. They are packed up in a wooden box, without any sort of preparation, one preffed upon another. The person who receives them, cuts off a little bit of the stalk, and steeps them for two hours in vinegar and water, when they recover their full bloom and beauty. Then he places them in water-bottles, in an apartment where they are screened from the severities of the weather: and they will continue fresh and unfaded, the best part of a month.

Amidst the plantations in the neighbourhood of Nice, appear a vast number of white *bastides*, or country-houses, which make a dazzling shew. Some few of these are good villas, belonging to the noblesse of this country; and even some of the bourgeois are provided with pretty lodgeable *cassines*; but, in general, they are the habitations of the peasants, and contain nothing but misery and vermin. They are built square; and being whitened with lime and plaister, contribute greatly to the richness of the view. The hills are shaded to the tops with olive-trees, which are always green; and those hills are o-ver-topped by more distant mountains, covered with snow. When I turn myself towards the sea, the view is bounded by the horizon; yet, in a clear morning, one can perceive the high lands of Corsica. On the right hand, it is terminated by Antibes, and the mountain of Esterelles, which I described in my last. As for the weather, you will conclude, from what I have said of the oranges, flowers, &c. that it must be wonderfully mild and serene: but of the climate I shall speak hereafter. Let me only observe, *en passant*, that the houses in general have no chimnies but in their kitchens; and that many people, even of condition, at Nice have no fire in their chambers during the whole winter. When the weather hap

LETTER XIII.

pens to be a little more sharp than usual, they warm their apartments with a *brasiere* of charcoal.

Though Nice itself retains few marks of ancient splendor, there are considerable monuments of antiquity in its neighbourhood. About two short miles from the town, upon the summit of a pretty high hill, we find the ruins of the ancient city Cemenelion, now called Cimia, which was once the metropolis of the maratime Alps, and the seat of a Roman president. With respect to situation, nothing could be more agreeable or salubrious. It stood upon the gentle ascent and summit of a hill, fronting the Mediterranean, from the shore of which it is distant about half a league; and, on the other side, it overlooked a bottom, or narrow vale, through which the Paglion (anciently called Paulo) runs towards the walls of Nice. It was inhabited by a people whom Ptolomy and Pliny call the *Vedantii*, but these were undoubtedly mixed with a Roman colony, as appears by the monuments which still remain; I mean the ruins of an amphitheatre, a temple of Apollo, baths, aqueducts, sepulchral and other stones, with inscriptions, and a great number of medals, which the peasants have found by accident, in digging and labouring the vineyards and corn-fields which now cover the ground where the city stood. Touching this city very little is to be learned from the ancient historians: but that it was the seat of a Roman præses, is proved by the two following inscriptions, which are still extant.

P. AELIO. SEVERINO.
V. E. P.
PRAESIDI. OPTIMO.
ORDO. CEMEN.
PATRONO.

This is now in the possession of the count de Gubernatis, who has a country house upon the spot. The other, found near the same place, is in praise of the præses Marcus Aurelius Masculus.

M. AVRELIO. MASCVLO.
V. E.
OB. EXIMIAM. PRAESIDATVS
EIVS. INTEGRITATEM. ET
EGREGIAM. AD. OMNES. HOMINE
MANSVETVDINEM. ET. VRGENTI
ANNONAE. SINCERAM. PRAEBI
TIONEM.
AC. MVNIFICENTIAM. ET. QVOI
AQVAE.
VSVM. VETVSTATE. LAPSVM. RI
QVISITVM. AC. REPERTVM. SAECV
FELICITATE. CVRSVI. PRISTINO

LETTER XIII.

REDDIDERIT.
COLLEG. III.
QVIB. EX. SCC. P. EST.
PATRONO. DIGNISS.

This president well deserved such a mark of respect from a people whom he had assisted in two such essential articles, as their corn and their water. You know, the præses of a Roman provence had the *jus figendi clavi*, the privilege of wearing the *latus clavus*, the *gladius, infula, prætexta, purpura, et annulus aureus*: he had his *vasa, vehicula, apparitores, Scipio eburneus, et sella curulis*.

I shall give you one more sepulchral inscription on a marble, which is now placed over the gate of the church belonging to the convent of St Pont, a venerable building, which stands at the bottom of the hill, fronting the north side of the town of Nice. This St Pont, or Pontius, was a Roman convert to Christianity, who suffered martyrdom at Cemenelion in the year 261, during the reigns of the emperors Valerian and Gallienus. The legends recount some ridiculous miracles wrought in favour of this saint, both before and after his death. Charels V. emperor of Germany and king of Spain, caused this monastery to be built on the spot where Pontius suffered decapitation. But to return to the inscription: it appears in these words.

LETTER XIII.

M. M. A.
FLAVIAE. BASILLAE. CONIVG. CARISSIM.
DOM. ROMA. MIRAE. ERGA. MARITVM.
AMORIS.
ADQ. CASTITAT. FAEMINAE QVAE. VIXIT
ANN. XXXV. M. III. DIEB XII. AVRELIVS
RHODISMANVS. AVG. LIB. COMMEM. ALP.
MART. ET AVRELIA ROMVLA. FILIA.
IMPATIENTISSIM. DOLOR. EIVS ADFLICTI
ADQ. DESOLATI. CARISSIM AC. MERENT.
FERET.
FEC. ET. DED.

The amphitheatre of Cemenelion is but very small, compared to that of Nismes. The arena is ploughed up, and bears corn; some of the seats remain, and part of two opposite porticos; but all the columns, and the external facade of the building, are taken away; so that it is impossible to judge of the architecture: all that we can perceive is, that it was built in an oval form. About one hundred paces from the amphitheatre stood an ancient temple, supposed to have been dedicated to Appollo. The original roof is demolished, as well as the portico; the vestiges of which may still be traced. The part called the Basilica, and about one half of the Cella Sanctior, remain, and are converted into the dwelling-house and stable of the peasant who takes care of the count de Gubernatis's garden, in which this monument stands. In the Cella Sanctior I found a lean cow, a he-goat, and a jack-afs; the very fame conjunction of animals which I had feen drawing a plough in Burgundy. Several mutilated ftatues have been dug up from the ruins of this temple, and a great number of medals have been found in the different vineyards which now occupy the fpace upon which ftood the ancient city of Cemenelion. Thefe were of gold, filver, and brafs. Many of them were prefented to Charles Emanuel I. duke of Savoy. The prince of Monaco has a good number of them in his collection; and the reft are in private hands. The peafants, in digging, have likewife found many urns, lachrimatories, and fepulchral ftones, with epitaphs, which are now difperfed among different convents and private houfes. All this ground is a rich mine of antiquities, which, if properly worked, would produce a great number of valuable curiofities. Juft by the temple of Apollo were the ruins of a bath, compofed of great blocks of marble, which have been taken away for the purpofes of modern building. In all probability, many other noble monuments of this city have been dilapidated by the fame barbarous œconomy. There are fome fubterranean vaults, through which the water was conducted to this bath, ftill extant on the garden of the count de Gubernatis. Of the aqueduct that conveyed water to the town, I can say very little, but that it was scooped through a mountain: that this subterranean passage was discovered some years ago, by removing the rubbish which choaked it up: that the people penetrating a considerable way, by the help of lighted torches, found a very plentiful stream of water flowing in an aqueduct as high as an ordinary man, arched over head, and lined with a sort of cement. They could not, however, trace this stream to its source; and it is again stopped up with earth and rubbish. There is not a soul in this country, who has either spirit or understanding to conduct an inquiry of this kind. Hard by the amphitheatre is a convent of Recollects, built in a very romantic situation, on the brink of a precipice. On one side of their garden they ascend a kind of esplanade, which they say was part of the citadel of Cemenelion. They have planted it with cypress trees, and flowering-shrubs. One of the monks told me that it was vaulted below, as they can plainly perceive by the sound of their instruments used in houghing the ground. A very small expence would bring the secrets of this cavern to light. The have nothing to do but to make a breach in the wall, which appears uncovered towards the garden.

The city of Cemenelion was first sacked by the Longobards, who made an irruption into Provence, under their king Alboinus, about the middle of the sixth century. It was afterwards totally destroyed by the Saracens, who, at different times, ravaged this whole coast. The remains of the people are supposed to have changed their habitation, and formed a coalition with the inhabitants of Nice.

What further I have to say of Nice, you shall know in good time; at present I have nothing to add, but what you very well know, that I am always your affectionate humble servant.

LETTER XIV.

Nice, January 20, 1764.

DEAR SIR,

LAST Sunday I crossed Montalban on horseback, with some Swiss officers, on a visit to our consul Mr B———d, who lives at Ville Franche, about half a league from Nice. It is a small town, built upon the side of a rock, at the bottom of the harbour, which is a fine basin, surrounded with hills on every side, except to the south, where it lyes open to the sea. If there was a small island in the mouth of it, to break off the force of the waves when the wind is southerly, it would be one of the finest harbours in the world; for the ground is exceeding good for anchorage: there is a sufficient depth of water, and room enough for the whole navy of England. On the right hand, as you enter the port, there is an elegant fanal, or light-house, kept in good repair. But in all the charts of this coast which I have seen, this lanthorn is laid down to the westward of the harbour; an error equally absurd and dangerous, as it may mislead the navigator, and induce him to run his ship among the rocks to the eastward of the light-house, where it would undoubtedly perish. Opposite to the mouth of the harbour is the fort, which can be of no service but in defending the shipping and the town by sea; for, by land, it is commanded by Montalban, and all the hills in the neighbourhood. In the war of 1744, it was taken and retaken. At present it is in tolerable good repair. On the left of the fort is the basin for the gallies, with a kind of dock, in which they are built, and occasionally laid up to be refitted. This basin is formed by a pretty stone mole; and here his Sardinian majesty's two gallies lye perfectly secure, moored with their sterns close to the jet te. I went on board one of these vessels, and saw about two hundred miserable wretches, chained to the banks, on which they sit and row, when the galley is at sea. This is a sight which a British subject, sensible of the blessing he enjoys, cannot behold without horror and compassion. Not but that if we consider the nature of the case with coolness and deliberation, we must acknowledge the justice, and even sagacity, of employing for the service of the public those malefactors who have forfeited their title to the privileges of the community. Among the slaves at Ville Franche is a Piedmontese count, condemned to the gallies for life, in consequence of having been convicted of forgery.

He is permitted to live on shore; and gets money by employing the other slaves to knit stockings for sale. He appears always in the Turkish habit, and is in a fair way of raising a better fortune than that which he has forfeited. It is a great pity, however, and a manifest outrage against the law of nations, as well as of humanity, to mix with those banditti, the Moorish and Turkish prisoners who are taken in the prosecution of open war. It is certainly no justification of this barbarous practice, that the Christian prisoners are treated as cruelly at Tunis and Algiers. It would be for the honour of Christendom there was a small island in the mouth of it, to break off the force of the waves when the wind is southerly, it would be one of the finest harbours in the world; for the ground is exceeding good for anchorage: there is a sufficient depth of water, and room enough for the whole navy of England. On the right hand, as you enter the port, there is an elegant fanal, or light-house, kept in good repair. But in all the charts of this coast which I have seen, this lanthorn is laid down to the westward of the harbour; an error equally absurd and dangerous, as it may mislead the navigator, and induce him to run his ship among the rocks to the eastward of the light-house, where it would undoubtedly perish. Opposite to the mouth of the harbour is the fort, which can be of no service but in defending the shipping and the town by sea; for, by land, it is commanded by Montalban, and all the hills in the neighbourhood. In the war of 1744, it was taken and retaken. At present it is in tolerable good repair. On the left of the fort is the basin for the gallies, with a kind of dock, in which they are built, and occasionally laid up to be refitted. This basin is formed by a pretty stone mole; and here his Sardinian majesty's two gallies lye perfectly secure, moored with their sterns close to the jet-te. I went on board one of these vessels, and saw about two hundred miserable wretches, chained to the banks, on which they sit and row, when the galley is at sea. This is a sight which a British subject, sensible of the blessing he enjoys, cannot behold without horror and compassion. Not but that if we consider the nature of the case with coolness and deliberation, we must acknowledge the justice, and even sagacity, of employing for the service of the public those malefactors who have forfeited their title to the privileges of the community. Among the slaves at Ville Franche is a Piedmontese count, condemned to the gallies for life, in consequence of having been convicted of forgery.

He is permitted to live on shore; and gets money by employing the other slaves to knit stockings for sale. He appears always in the Turkish habit, and is in a fair way of raising a better fortune than that which he has forfeited. It is a great pity, however, and a manifest outrage against the law of nations, as well as of humanity, to mix with those banditti, the Moorish and Turkish prisoners who are taken in the prosecution of open war. It is certainly no justification of this barbarous practice, that the Christian prisoners are treated as cruelly at Tunis and Algiers. It would be for the honour of Christendom to set an example of generosity to the Turks: and, if they would not follow it, to join their naval forces, and extirpate at once those nests of pirates, who have so long infested the Mediterranean. Certainly, nothing can be more shameful, than the treaties which France and the Maritime powers have concluded with those barbarians. They supply them with artillery, arms, and ammunition, to disturb their neighbours. They even pay them a sort of tribute, under the denomination of presents; and often put up with insults tamely, for the sordid consideration of a little gain in the way of commerce. They know that Spain, Sardinia, and almost all the Catholic powers in the Mediterranean, Adriatic, and Levant, are at perpetual war with those Mahometans; that while Algiers, Tunis and Sallee maintain armed cruisers at sea, those Christian powers will not run the risque of trading in their own bottoms, but rather employ as carriers the maritime nations who are at peace with the infidels It is for our share of this advantage, that we cultivate the piratical states of Barbary, and meanly purchase passports of them, thus acknowledging them masters of the Mediterranean.

The Sardinian gallies are mounted each with five-and-twenty oars, and six guns, six-pounders, of a side, and a large piece of artillery a midships, pointing a-head, which (so far as I am able to judge) can never be used point-blank, without demolishing the head or prow of the galley. The accommodation on board for the officers is wretched. There is a paltry cabin in the poop for the commander; but all the other officers lye below the slaves, in a dungeon, where they have neither light, air, nor any degree of quiet; half suffocated by the heat of the place; tormented by fleas, bugs and lice, and disturbed by the incessant noise over head. The slaves lye upon the naked banks, without any other covering than a tilt. This, however, is no great hardship, in a climate where there is scarce any winter. They are fed with a very scanty allowance of bread, and about fourteen beans a day; and twice a week they have a little rice, or cheese; but most of them, while they are in harbour, knit stockings, or do some other kind of work, which enables them to make some addition to this wretched allowance. When they happen to be at sea in bad weather, their situation is truly deplorable. Every wave breaks over the vessel, and not only keeps them continually wet, but comes with such force, that they are dashed against the banks with surprising violence: sometimes their limbs are broke, and sometimes their brains dashed out. It is impossible (they say) to keep such a number of desperate people under any regular command, without exercising such severities as must shock humanity. It is almost equally impossible to maintain any tolerable degree of cleanliness, where such a number of wretches are crouded together without conveniences, or even the necessaries of life. They are ordered twice a week to strip, clean, and bathe themselves in the sea: but, notwithstanding all the precautions of discipline, they swarm with vermin, and the vessel smells like an hospital, or crouded jail. They seem nevertheless, quite insensible of their misery, like so many convicts in Newgate: they laugh and sing, and swear, and get drunk when they can. When you enter by the stern, you are welcomed by a band of music selected from the slaves; and these expect a gratification. If you walk forwards, you must take care of your pockets. You will be accosted by one or other of the slaves, with a brush and blacking-ball for cleaning your shoes; and if you undergo this operation, it is ten to one but your pocket is picked. If you decline his service, and keep aloof, you will find it almost impossible to avoid a colony of vermin, which these fellows have a very dextrous method of conveying to strangers. Some of the Turkish prisoners, whose ransom or exchange is expected, are allowed to go ashore, under proper inspection; and those *forcats*, who have served the best part of the time for which they were condemned, are employed in public works, under a guard of soldiers. At the harbour of Nice, they are hired by ship-masters to bring ballast, and have a small proportion of what they earn, for their own use: the rest belongs to the king. They are distinguished by an iron shackle about one of their legs. The road from Nice to Ville-franche is scarce passable on horseback: a circumstance the more extraordinary, as those slaves, in the space of two or three months, might even make it fit for a carriage, and the king would not be one farthing out of pocket, for they are quite idle the greatest part of the year.

The gallies go to sea only in the summer. In tempestuous weather, they could not live out of port. Indeed they are good for nothing but in smooth water, during a calm; when, by dint of rowing they make good way. The king of Sardinia is so sensible of their inutility, that he intends to let his gallies rot; and, in lieu of them, has purchased two large frigates in England, one of fifty, and another of thirty guns, which are now in the harbour of Ville-franche. He has also procured an English officer, one Mr A——, who is second in command on board one of them, and has the title of captain *consulteur*, that is, instructor to the first captain, the Marquis de M———i, who knows as little of seamanship as I do of Arabic.

The king, it is said, intends to have two or three more frigates, and then he will be more than a match for the Barbary corsairs, provided care be taken to man his fleet in a proper manner. But this will never be done, unless he invites foreigners into his service, officers as well as seamen; for his own dominions produce neither at present. If he is really determined to make the most of the maritime situation of his dominions, as well as of his alliance with Great Britain, he ought to supply his ships with English mariners, and put a British commander at the head of his fleet. He ought to erect magazines and docks at Ville-franche; or, if there is not conveniency for building, he may at least have pits and wharfs for heaving down and careening; and these ought to be under the direction of Englishmen, who best understand all the particulars of marine œconomy. Without all doubt, he will not be able to engage foreigners, without giving them liberal appointments; and their being engaged in his service will give umbrage to his own subjects: but, when the business is to establish a maritime power, these considerations ought to be sacrificed to reasons of public utility. Nothing can be more absurd and unreasonable than the murmurs of the Piedmontese officers at the preferment of foreigners, who execute those things for the advantage of their country, of which they know themselves incapable. When Mr P―――n was first promoted in the service of his Sardinian Majesty, he met with great opposition, and numberless mortifications, from the jealousy of the Piedmontese officers, and was obliged to hazard his life on many rencounters with them, before they would be quiet. Being a man of uncommon spirit, he never suffered the least insult or affront to pass unchastised. He had repeated opportunities of signalising his valour against the Turks; and by dint of extraordinary merit, and long services, not only attained the chief command of the gallies, with the rank of lieutenant-general, but also acquired a very considerable share of the king's favour, and was appointed commandant of Nice.

LETTER XIV.

His Sardinian majesty found his account more ways than one, in thus promoting Mr P——n. He made the acquisition of an excellent officer, of tried courage and fidelity, by whose advice he conducted his marine affairs. This gentleman was perfectly well esteemed at the court of London. In the war of 1744, he lived in the utmost harmony with the British admirals who commanded our fleet in the Mediterranean. In consequence of this good understanding, a thousand occasional services were performed by the English ships, for the benefit of his master, which otherwise could not have been done, without a formal application to our ministry; in which case, the opportunities would have been lost. I know our admirals had general orders and instructions to co-operate in all things with his Sardinian majesty; but I know, also, by experience, how little these general instructions avail, when the admiral is not cordially interested in the service. Were the king of Sardinia at present engaged with England in a new war against France, and a British squadron stationed upon this coast, as formerly, he would find a great difference in this particular. He should therefore carefully avoid having at Nice a Savoyard commandant, utterly ignorant of sea-affairs, unacquainted with the true interest of his master, proud and arbitrary, reserved to strangers, from a prejudice of national jealousy, and particularly averse to the English.

With respect to the ancient name of Villa-franca, there is a dispute among antiquarians. It is not at all mentioned in the *Itenerarium* of Antoninus, unless it is meant as the port of Nice. But it is more surprising that the accurate Strabo, in describing this coast, mentions no such harbour, Some people imagine, it is the Portus Herculis Monæci. But this is undoubtedly what is now called *Monaco;* the harbour of which exactly tallies with what Strabo says of the Portus Monæci—*neque magnas, neque multas capit navis.* Ptolemy, indeed, seems to mention it under the name of Herculis Portus, different from the Portus Monæci. His words are these: *Post vari ostium ad Ligustrium mare, Massiliensium sunt* Nicæa, *Herculis Portus, Trophæa Augusti, Monæci Portus.* In that case, Hercules was worshipped both here and at Monaco, and gave his name to both places. But on this subject I shall perhaps speak more fully in another letter, after I have seen the *Trophæa Augusti,* now called *Tourbia,* and the town of Monaco, which last is about three leagues from Nice. Here I cannot help taking notice of the following elegant description from the

Pharsalia, which seems to have been intended for this very harbour.

Finis et Hesperiæ promoto milite varus,
Quaque sub Herculeo sacratus numine portus
Urget rupe cava pelagus, non Corus *in illum*
Jus habet, aut Zephyrus, *solus sua littora turbat*
Circius, *et tuta prohibet statione Monæci.*

The present town of Villa-franca was built and settled in the thirteenth century, by order of Charles II. king of the Sicilies, and count of Provence, in order to defend the harbour from the descents of the Saracens, who at that time infested the coast. The inhabitants were removed hither from another town, situated on the top of a mountain in the neighbourhood, which those pirates had destroyed. Some ruins of the old town are still extant. In order to secure the harbour still more effectually, Emanuel Philibert, duke of Savoy, built the fort in the beginning of the last century, together with the mole where the gallies are moored. As I said before, Ville-franche is built on the face of a barren rock, washed by the sea; and there is not an acre of plain ground within a mile of it. In summer the reflexion of the sun from the rocks must make it intolerably hot; for even at this time of the year I walked myself into a profuse sweat, by going about a quarter of a mile to see the gallies.

Pray remember me to our friends at A——'s, and believe me to be ever yours.

LETTER XV.

Nice, January 3 1764.

MADAM,

IN your favour which I received by Mr M——l, you remind me of my promise, to communicate the remarks I have still to make on the French nation; and at the same time you signify your opinion, that I am too severe in my former observations. You even hint a suspicion, that this severity is owing to some personal cause of resentment: but I protest I have no particular cause of animosity against any individual of that country. I have neither obligation to, nor quarrel with, any subject of France; and when I meet with a Frenchman worthy of my esteem, I can receive him into my friendship, with as much cordiality as I could feel for any fellow-citizen of the same merit. I even respect the nation, for the number of great men it has produced in all arts and sciences. I respect the French officers, in particular, for their gallantry and valour; and especially for that generous humanity which they exercise towards their enemies, even amidst the horrors of war. This liberal spirit is the only circumstance of antient chivalry which I think was worth preserving. It had formerly flourished in England, but was almost extinguished in a succession of civil wars, which are always productive of cruelty and rancour. It was Henry IV. of France, (a real knight errant,) who revived it in Europe. He possessed that greatness of mind which can forgive injuries of the deepest dye. and as he had also the faculty of distinguishing characters, he found his account in favouring with his friendship and confidence some of those who had opposed him in the field with the most inveterate perseverance. I know not whether he did more service to mankind in general, by reviving the practice of treating his prisoners with generosity, than he prejudised his own country by patronizing the absurd and pernicious custom of duelling, and establishing a *punto*, founded in diametrical opposition to common sense and humanity.

I have often heard it observed, that a French officer is generally an agreeable companion when he is turned of fifty. Without all doubt, by that time, the fire of his vivacity, which makes him so troublesome in his youth, will be considerably abated, and in other respects he must be improved by his experience. But there is a fundamental error in the first principles of his education, which time rather confirms than removes. Early prejudices are for the most part converted into habits of thinking; and accordingly you will find the old officers in the French service more bigoted than their juniors to the punctilios of false honour.

A lad of a good family no sooner enters into the service, than he thinks it incumbent upon him to shew his courage in a rencontre. His natural vivacity prompts him to hazard in company every thing that comes uppermost, without any respect to his seniors or betters; and ten to one but he says something which he finds it necessary to maintain with his sword. The old officer, instead of checking his petulance, either by rebuke or silent disapprobation, seems to be pleased with his impertinence, and encourages every sally of his presumption. Should a quarrel ensue, and the parties go out, he makes no efforts to compromise the dispute; but sits with a pleasing expectation to learn the issue of the rencontre. If the young man is wounded, he kisses him with transport, extols his bravery, puts him into the hands of the surgeon, and visits him with great tenderness every day, until he is cured. If he is killed on the spot, he shrugs up his shoulders—says, *Quelle dommage! c' etoit un aimable enfant! ah, patience!* and in three hours the defunct is forgotten. You know, in France, duels are forbid on pain of death; but this law is easily evaded. The person insulted walks out, the antagonist understands the hint, and follows him into the street, where they justle as if by accident, draw their swords, and one of them is either killed or disabled, before any effectual means can be used to part them. Whatever may be the issue of the combat, the magistrate takes no cognizance of it; at least, it is interpreted into an accidental rencounter, and no penalty is incurred on either side. Thus the purpose of the law is entirely defeated, by a most ridiculous and cruel connivance. The meerest trifles in conversation, a rash word, a distant hint, even a look or smile of contempt, is sufficient to produce one of these combats; but injuries of a deeper dye, such as terms of reproach, the lie direct, a blow, or even the menace of a blow, must be discussed with more formality. In any of these cases, the parties agree to meet in the dominions of another prince, where they can murder each other without fear of punishment. An officer who is struck, or even threatened with a blow must not be quiet, until he either kills his antagonist, or loses his own life. A friend of mine, (a Niſſard,) who was in the service of France, told me, that some years ago one of their captains, in the heat of passion, struck his lieutenant. They fought immediately: the lieutenant was wounded and disarmed. As it was an affront that could not be made up, he no sooner recovered of his wounds, than he called out the captain a second time. In a word, they fought five times before the combat proved decisive; at last, the lieutenant was left dead on the spot. This was an event which sufficiently proved the absurdity of the punctilio that gave rise to it. The poor gentleman who was insulted and outraged by the brutality of the aggressor, found himself under the necessity of giving him a further occasion to take away his life. Another adventure of the same kind happened a few years ago in this place. A French officer having threatened to strike another, a formal challenge ensued; and it being agreed that they should fight until one of them dropped, each provided himself with a couple of pioneers to dig his grave on the spot. They engaged just without one of the gates of Nice, in presence of a great number of spectators, and fought with surprising fury, until the ground was drenched with their blood. At length, one of them stumbled, and fell; upon which the other, who found himself mortally wounded, advancing, and dropping his point, said, " *Je te donne ce que tu m' as ôté.*" " I give thee that which thou haſt taken from me." So ſaying, he dropped dead upon the field. The other, who had been the perſon inſulted, was ſo dangerouſly wounded that he could not riſe. Some of the ſpectators carried him forthwith to the beach, and putting him into a boat, conveyed him by ſea to Antibes. The body of his antagoniſt was denied Chriſtian burial, as he died without abſolution, and every body allowed that his ſoul went to hell: but the gentlemen of the army declared that he died like a man of honour. Should a man be never ſo well inclined to make atonement in a peaceable manner, for an inſult given in the heat of paſſion, or in the fury of intoxication, it cannot be received. Even an involuntary treſpaſs from ignorance, or abſence of mind, muſt be cleanſed with blood. A certain noble lord of our country, when he was yet a commoner, on his travels, involved himſelf in a dilemma of this ſort, at the court of Lorrain. He had been riding out; and ſtrolling along a public walk, in a brown ſtudy, with his horſewhip in his hand, perceived a caterpillar crawling on the back of a marquis, who chanced to be before him. He never thought of the *petit maitre;* but lifting up his whip, in order to kill the insect, laid it across his shoulders with a crack that alarmed all the company in the walk. The marquis's sword was produced in a moment, and the aggressor in great hazard of his life, as he had no weapon of defence. He was no sooner waked from his reverie, than he begged pardon, and offered to make all proper concessions for what he had done through mere inadvertency. The marquis would have admitted his excuses, had there been any precedent of such an affront washed away without blood. A conclave of honour was immediately assembled; and after long disputes, they agreed, that an involuntary offence, especially from *such a kind of man, d'un tel homme,* might be atoned by concessions. That you may have some idea of the small beginning from which many gigantic quarrels arise, I shall recount one that lately happened at Lyons, as I had it from the mouth of a person who was an ear and eye-witness of the transaction. Two Frenchmen, at a public ordinary, stunned the rest of the company with their loquacity. At length one of them, with a supercilious air, asked the other's name. "I never tell my name, (said he,) but in a whisper." "You may have very good reasons for keeping it secret," replied the first. "I will tell you," (resumed the other:) with these words, he rose; and going round to him, pronounced, loud enough to be heard by the whole company, "*Je m' appelle Pierre Pysan; et vous etes un impertinent.*" So saying, he walked out: the interrogator followed him into the street, where they justled, drew their swords, and engaged. He who asked the question was run through the body; but his relations were so powerful, that the victor was obliged to fly his own country. He was tried and condemned in his absence, his goods were confiscated; his wife broke her heart; his children were reduced to beggary; and he himself is now starving in exile. In England we have not yet adopted all the implacability of the punctilio. A gentleman may be insulted even with a blow, and survive, after having once hazarded his life against the aggressor. The laws of honour in our country do not oblige him either to slay the person from whom he received the injury, or even to fight to the last drop of his own blood. One finds no examples of duels among the Romans, who were certainly as brave and as delicate in their notions of honour, as the French. Cornelius Nepos tells us, that a famous Athenian general having a dispute with his colleague, who was of Sparta, a man of a fiery disposition, this last lifted up his cane to strike him. Had this happened to a French *petit maitre*, death must have ensued. but mark what followed. ——The Athenian, far from resenting the outrage in what is now called a gentleman-like manner, said, " Do, strike if you please; but hear me." He never dreamed of cutting the Lacedemonian's throat; but bore with his passionate temper, as the infirmity of a friend who had a thousand good qualities to overbalance that defect.

I need not expatiate upon the folly and the mischief which are countenanced and promoted by the modern practice of duelling. I need not give examples of friends who have murdered each other, in obedience to this savage custom, even while their hearts were melting with mutual tenderness; nor will I particularize the instances which I myself know, of whole families ruined, of women and children made widows and orphans, of parents deprived of only sons, and of valuable lives lost to the community, by duels, which had been produced by one unguarded expression, uttered without intention of offence, in the heat of dispute and altercation. I shall not insist upon the hardship of a worthy man's being obliged to devote himself to death, because it is his misfortune to be insulted by a brute, a bully, a drunkard, or a madman: neither will I enlarge upon this side of the absurdity, which indeed amounts to a contradiction in terms; I mean the dilemma to which a gentleman of the army is reduced when he receives an affront. if he does not challenge and fight his antagonist, he is broke with infamy by a court-martial; if he fights and kills him, he is tried by the civil power, convicted of murder, and, if the royal mercy does not interpose, he is infallibly hanged; all this, exclusive of the risque of his own life in the duel, and his conscience being burdened with the blood of a man, whom perhaps he has sacrificed to a false punctilio, even contrary to his own judgment. These are reflections which I know your own good sense will suggest. But I will make bold to propose a remedy for this gigantic evil, which seems to gain ground every day. let a court be instituted for taking cognizance of all breaches of honour, with power to punish by fine, pillory, sentence of infamy, outlawry, and exile, by virtue of an act of parliament made for this purpose; and all persons insulted, shall have recourse to this tribunal. let every man who seeks personal reparation with sword, pistol, or other instrument of death, be declared infamous, and banished the kingdom: let every man convicted of having used a sword or pistol, or other mortal weapon against another, either in duel or rencountre, occasioned by any previous quarrel, be subject to the same penalties: if any man is killed in a duel, let his body be hanged upon a public gibbet for a certain time, and then given to the surgeons: let his antagonist be hanged as a murderer, and dissected also; and some mark of infamy be set on the memory of both. I apprehend such regulations would put an effectual stop to the practice of duelling, which nothing but the fear of infamy can support; for I am persuaded, that no being, capable of reflection, would prosecute the trade of assassination at the risque of his own life, if this hazard was, at the same time reinforced by the certain prospect of infamy and ruin. Every person of sentiment would in that case allow, that an officer who in a duel robs a deserving woman of her husband, a number of children of their father, a family of its support, and the community of a fellow-citizen, has as little merit to plead from exposing his own person, as a highwayman or housebreaker, who every day risques his life to rob or plunder that which is not of half the importance to society. I think it was from the Buccaneers of America that the English have learned to abolish one solecism in the practice of duelling: those adventurers decided their personal quarrels with piſtols; and this improvement has been adopted in Great Britain with good ſucceſs; though in France, and other parts of the continent, it is looked upon as a proof of their barbarity. It is, however, the only circumſtance of duelling which favours of common ſenſe, as it puts all mankind upon a level, the old with the young, the weak with the ſtrong, the unwieldy with the nimble, and the man who knows not how to hold a ſword with the *ſpadaſſin* who has practiſed fencing from the cradle. What glory is there in a man's vanquiſhing an adverſary over whom he has a manifeſt advantage? To abide the iſſue of a combat in this caſe, does not even require that moderate ſhare of reſolution which nature has indulged to her common children. Accordingly, we have ſeen ſo many inſtances of a coward's provoking a man of honour to battle. In the reign of our ſecond Charles, when duels flouriſhed in all their abſurdity, and the ſeconds fought while their principals were engaged, Villiers Duke of Buckingham, not content with having debauched the counteſs of Shrewſbury, and publiſhing her ſhame, took all opportunities of provoking the earl to ſingle combat, hoping he ſhould have an eaſy conqueſt. his lordſhip being a puny little creature, quiet, inoffenſive, and every way unfit for ſuch personal contests. He ridiculed him on all occasions; and at last declared in public company, that there was no glory in cuckolding Shrewsbury, who had not spirit to resent the injury. This was an insult which could not be overlooked. The earl sent him a challenge; and they agreed to fight, at Barns-elms, in presence of two gentlemen whom they chuse for their seconds. All the four engaged at the same time: the first thrust was fatal to the earl of Shrewsbury; and his friend killed the Duke's second at the same instant. Buckingham, elated with his exploit, set out immediately for the earl's seat at Cliefden, where he lay with his wife, after having boasted of the murder of her husband, whose blood he shewed her upon his sword, as a trophy of his prowess. But this very duke of Buckingham was little better than a paltroon at bottom. When the gallant earl of Ossory challenged him to fight in Chelsea-fields, he crossed the water to Batersea, where he pretended to wait for his lordship; and then complained to the house of Lords, that Ossory had given him the rendezvous, and did not keep his appointment. He knew the house would interpose in the quarrel, and he was not disappointed. Their lordships obliged them both to give their word quarrels with piſtols; and this improvement has been adopted in Great Britain with good ſucceſs; though in France, and other parts of the continent, it is looked upon as a proof of their barbarity. It is, however, the only circumſtance of duelling which favours of common ſenſe, as it puts all mankind upon a level, the old with the young, the weak with the ſtrong, the unwieldy with the nimble, and the man who knows not how to hold a ſword with the *ſpadaſſin* who has practiſed fencing from the cradle. What glory is there in a man's vanquiſhing an adverſary over whom he has a manifeſt advantage? To abide the iſſue of a combat in this caſe, does not even require that moderate ſhare of reſolution which nature has indulged to her common children. Accordingly, we have ſeen ſo many inſtances of a coward's provoking a man of honour to battle. In the reign of our ſecond Charles, when duels flouriſhed in all their abſurdity, and the ſeconds fought while their principal were engaged, Villiers Duke of Buckingham, not content with having debauched the counteſs of Shrewſbury, and publiſhing her ſhame, took all opportunities of provoking the earl to ſingle combat, hoping he ſhould have an eaſy conqueſt, his lordſhip being a puny little creature, quite inoffenſive, and every way unfit for ſuc personal contests. He ridiculed him on all occasions; and at last declared in public company, that there was no glory in cuckolding Shrewsbury, who had not spirit to resent the injury. This was an insult which could not be overlooked. The earl sent him a challenge; and they agreed to fight, at Barns-elms, in presence of two gentlemen whom they chuse for their seconds. All the four engaged at the same time: the first thrust was fatal to the earl of Shrewsbury; and his friend killed the duke's second at the same instant. Buckingham, elated with his exploit, set out immediately for the earl's seat at Cliefden, where he lay with his wife, after having boasted of the murder of her husband, whose blood he shewed her upon his sword, as a trophy of his prowess. But this very duke of Buckingham was little better than a paltroon at bottom. When the gallant earl of Ossory challenged him to fight in Chelsea-fields, he crossed the water to Batersea, where he pretended to wait for his lordship; and then complained to the house of Lords, that Ossory had given him the rendezvous, and did not keep his appointment. He knew the house would interpose in the quarrel, and he was not disappointed. Their lordships obliged them both to give their word of honour that their quarrel should have no other consequences.

I ought to make an apology for having troubled a lady with so many observations on a subject so unsuitable to the softness of the fair sex; but I know you cannot be indifferent to any thing that so nearly affects the interests of humanity, which I can safely aver have alone suggested every thing which has been said by,

  Madam,

    Your very humble servant.

LETTER XVI.

Nice, May 2, 1764.

DEAR DOCTOR,

A Few days ago I rode out with two gentlemen of this country, to see a stream of water which was formerly conveyed in an aqueduct to the ancient city of Cemenelion, from whence this place is distant about a mile, though separated by abrupt rocks and deep hollows, which last are here honoured with the name of vallies. The water, which is exquisitely cool, and light and pure, gushes from the middle of a rock, by a hole which lead to a subterranean aqueduct carried through the middle of the mountain. This is a Roman work, and the more I considered it, appeared the more stupendous. A peasant who lives upon the spot told us, he had entered by this hole at eight in the morning, and advanced so far, that it was four in the afternoon before he came out. He said he walked in the water, through a regular canal formed of a hard stone, lined with a kind of cement, and vaulted over-head; but so high in most parts he could stand upright, yet in others the bed of the canal was so filled with earth and stones that he was obliged to stoop in passing. He said that there were air-holes at certain distances, (and indeed I saw one of these not far from the present issue;) that there were some openings and stone seats on the sides, and here and there figures of men formed of stone, with hammers and working tools in their hands. I am apt to believe the fellow romanced a little, in order to render his adventure the more marvellous: but I am certainly informed, that several persons have entered this passage, and proceeded a considerable way by the light of torches, without arriving at the source, which, if we may believe the tradition of the country, is at the distance of eight leagues from this opening but this is altogether incredible. The stream is now called *la fontaine de muraille*, and is carefully conducted by different branches into the adjacent vineyards and gardens, for watering the ground. On the side of the same mountain, more southerly, at the distance of half a mile, there is another still more copious discharge of the same kind of water, called *la source du temple*. It was conveyed through the same kind of passage, and put to the same use as the other; and I should imagine they are both from the same source, which, though hitherto undiscovered, must be at a considerable distance as the mountain is continued for several leagues to the westward, without exhibiting the least signs of water in any other part. But, exclusive of the subterranean conduits, both these streams must have been conveyed through aqueducts extending from hence to Cemenelion over steep rocks and deep ravines, at a prodigious expence. The water from this *source du temple* issues from a stone building which covers the passage in the rock. It serves to turn several olive, corn, and paper mills, being conveyed through a modern aqueduct raised upon a paltry arcade at the expence of the public, and afterwards branched off in very small streams, for the benefit of this parched and barren country. The Romans were so used to bathing, that

LETTER XVI.

they could not exist without a great quantity of water; and this, I imagine, is one reason that induced them to spare no labour and expence in bringing it from a distance, when they had not plenty of it at home. But, besides this motive, they had another: they were so nice and delicate in their taste of water, that they took great pains to supply themselves with the purest and lightest from afar, for drinking and culinary uses, even while they had plenty of an inferior sort for their baths, and other domestic purposes. There are springs of good water on the spot where Cemenelion stood; but there is a hardness in all well-water, which quality is deposited in running a long course, especially if exposed to the influence of the sun and air. The Romans, therefore had good reason to soften and meliorate this element, by conveying it a good length of way in open aqueducts. What was used in the baths of Cemenelion, they probably brought in leaden pipes, some of which have been dug up very lately by accident. You must know, I made a second excursion to these ancient ruins, and measured the arena of the amphitheatre with packthread. It is an oval figure; the longest diameter extending to about one hundred and thirteen feet, and the shortest to eighty-eight; but I will not answer for the exactness of the measurement. In the centre of it, there was a square stone, with an iron ring, to which I suppose the wild beasts were tied, to prevent their springing upon the spectators. Some of the seats remain, with two opposite entrances, consisting each of one large gate, and two lateral smaller doors, arched there is also a considerable portion of the external wall; but no columns, or other ornaments of architecture. Hard by, in the garden of the count de Gubernatis, I saw the remains of a bath, fronting the portal of the temple, which I have described in a former letter; and here were some shafts of marble pillars, particularly a capital of the Corinthian order, beautifully cut, of white alabaster. Here the count found a large quantity of fine marble, which he has converted to various uses; and some mutilated statues, bronze as well as marble. The peasant shewed me some brass and silver medals, which he has picked up at different times in labouring the ground; together with several oblong beads of coloured glass, which were used as ear rings by the Roman ladies; and a small seal of agate, very much defaced. Two of the medals were of Maximian and Galienus; the rest were so consumed, that I could not read the legend. You know, that on public occa sions, such as games, and certain sacrifices, handfuls of medals were thrown among the people; a practice which accounts for the great number, which have been already found in this district. I saw some subterranean passages, which seemed to have been common-sewers, and a great number of old walls still standing along the brink of a precipice which overhangs the Paglion. The peasants tell me, that they never dig above a yard in depth, without finding vaults or cavities. All the vineyards and garden-grounds, for a considerable extent, are vaulted underneath; and all the ground that produces their grapes, fruit, and garden-stuff, is no more than the crumbled lime and rubbish of old Roman buildings, mixed with manure brought from Nice. This ancient town commanded a most noble prospect of the the sea; but is altogether innaccessible by any kind of wheel-carriage. If you make shift to climb to it on horseback, you cannot descend to the plain again, without running the risque of breaking your neck.

About seven or eight miles on the other side of Nice, are the remains of another Roman monument, which has greatly suffered from the barbarity of successive ages. It was a trophy erected by the senate of Rome, in honour of Augustus Cæsar, when he had totally subdued all the ferocious nations of these Maritime Alps, such as the Trumpilini Camuni, Vennonetes, Isnarci, Breuni, &c. It stands upon the top of a mountain which overlooks the town of Monaco, and now exhibits the appearance of an old ruined tower. There is a description of what it was, in an Italian manuscript, by which it appears to have been a beautiful edifice of two stories, adorned with columns and trophies in alto relievo, with a statue of Augustus Cæsar on the top. On one of the sides was an inscription, some words of which are still legible, upon the fragment of a marble found close to the old building: but the whole is preserved in Pliny, who gives it in these words, lib. iii cap. 20.

IMPERATORI CAESARI DIVI. F. AVG.
PONT.
MAX. IMP. XIV. TRIBVNIC. POTEST.
XVIII.
S. P. Q. R.
QVOD. EIVS DVCTI, AVSPICIISQ. GEN
TES ALPINAE OMNES, QVAE MARI
AD INFERVM PERTINEBANT, SVB IM
PERIVM PO. RO SVNT REDAC. GEN
TES ALPINAE DEVICTAE. TRVMPILIN
CAMVNI, VENNONETES, ISNARCI, BRI
VNI, NAVNES, FOCUNATES, VINDEL
CORVM GENTES QVATVOR, CONVI
NETES, VIRUCINATES, LICATES, C
TENATES, ABISONETES, RVGVSCI, S

LETTER XVI.

ANETES, CALVCONES, BRIXENTES, LEPONTII, VIBERI, NANTUATES, SEDVNI, VERAGRI, SALASSI, ACITAVONES MEDVLLI, VICINI, CATVRIGES, BRIGIANI, SOGIVNVI, EBRODVNTII, NEMALONES, EDENETES, ESVBIANI, VEAMINI, GALLITAE, TRIVLLATI, ECTINI, VERGVNNI, EGVITVRI, NEMENTVRI, ORATELLI, NERVSCI, VELAVNI, SVETRI.

Pliny, however, is mistaken in placing this inscription on a trophy near the *Augusta prætoria*, now called *Aosta* in Piedmont: where, indeed, there is a triumphal arch, but no inscription. This noble monument of antiquity was first of all destroyed by fire; and afterwards, in Gothic times, converted into a kind of fortification. The marbles belonging to it were either employed in adorning the church of the adjoining village ‡ which

---

‡ This was formerly a considerable town called *Villa Martis*, and pretends to the honour of having given birth to Aulus Helvius, who succeeded Commodus as emperor of Rome, by the name of Pertinax, which he acquired from his obstinate refusal of that dignity, when it was forced upon him by the senate. You know this man, though of very low birth, possessed many excellent qualities, and was basely murdered by the prætorian guards, at the instigation of Didius Julianus. For my part, I could never read without emotion, that celebrated eulogium of the senate, who exclaimed after his death, *Pertinate imperante, securi viximus, nen inem timuimus, patre pio, patro senatus, patre omnium bonorum.*

is still called *Turbia*, a corruption of *Trophæa*; or converted into tomb-stones, or carried off to be preserved in one or two churches of Nice. At present, the work has the appearance of a ruinous watch-tower, with Gothic battlements; and as such stands undistinguished by those who travel by sea from hence to Genoa, and other parts of Italy. I think I have now described all the antiquities in the neighbourhood of Nice, except some catacombs or caverns, dug in a rock at St Hospice, which Busching, in his geography, has described as a strong town and sea-port, though in fact there is not the least vestige either of town or village. It is a point of land almost opposite to the tower of Turbia, with the mountains of which it forms a bay, where there is a great and curious fishery of the tunny fish, farmed of the king of Sardinia. Upon this point there is a watch-tower still kept in repair, to give notice to the people in the neighbourhood, in case any Barbary corsairs should appear on the coast. The catacombs were in all probability dug, in former times, as places of retreat for the inhabitants upon sudden descents of the Saracens, who greatly infested these seas for several successive centuries. Many curious persons have entered them, and proceeded a considerable way by torch-light without arriving at the further extremity; and the tradition of the country is, that they reach as far as the ancient city of Cemenelion; but this is an idle suppofition, almoft as ridiculous as that which afcribes them to the labour and ingenuity of the fairies: they confift of narrow fubterranean paffages, vaulted with ftone, and lined with cement. Here and there one finds detached apartments like fmall chambers, where I fuppofe the people remained concealed till the danger was over. Diodorus Siculus tells us, that the ancient inhabitants of this country ufually lived under ground. " *Ligures in terra cubant ut plurimum; plures ad cava faxa speluncafque ab natura factas, ubi tegantur corpora, divertunt.*" This was likewife the cuftom of the Troglodytæ, a people bordering upon Ethiopia, who according to Ælian, lived in fubterranean caverns; from whence, indeed, they took their name ρωχλη, fignifying a cavern; and Virgil, in his Georgics, defcribes them thus:

" *Ipfi in defoffis fpecubus, fecura fub alta*
" *Ocia agunt terra.*"——

Thefe are dry fubjects; but fuch as the country affords. If we have not white paper, we muft fnow with brown. Even that which I am now fcrawling may be useful, if not entertaining: it is therefore the more confidently offered by,

Dear Sir,

Yours affectionately,

LETTER XVII.

Nice, July 2, 1764

DEAR SIR,

NICE was originally a colony from Marseilles. You know the Phocians (if we may believe Justin and Polybius) settled in Gaul, and built Marseilles, during the reign of Tarquinius Priscus at Rome. This city flourished to such a degree, that long before the Romans were in a condition to extend their dominion, it sent forth colonies, and established them along the coast of Liguria. Of these, Nice, or Nicæa, was one of the most remarkable; so called, in all probability, from the Greek word Νίκη, signifying *Victoria*, in consequence of some important victory obtained over the Salij and Ligures, who were the ancient inhabitants of this country. Nice, with its mother city, being in the sequel subdued by the Romans, fell afterwards successively under the dominion of the Goths

Burgundians, and Franks, the kings of Arles, and the kings of Naples, as counts of Provence. In the year one thousand three hundred and eighty-eight, the city and county of Nice being but ill protected by the family of Durazzo, voluntarily surrendered themselves to Amadæus, surnamed the Red, duke of Savoy; and since that period, they have continued as part of that potentate's dominions, except at such times as they have been over-run and possessed by the power of France, which hath always been a troublesome neighbour to this country. The castle was begun by the Arragonian counts of Provence, and afterwards enlarged by several successive dukes of Savoy, so as to be deemed impregnable, until the modern method of besieging began to take place. A fruitless attempt was made upon it in the year one thousand five hundred and forty-three, by the French and Turks in conjunction: but it was reduced several times after that period, and is now in ruins. The celebrated engineer Vauban, being commanded by Louis XIV. to give in a plan for fortifying Nice, proposed that the river Paglion should be turned into a new channel, so as to surround the town to the north, and fall into the harbour; that where the Paglion now runs, to the westward of the city-walls, there should be a deep ditch to be filled with sea-water; and that a fortress should be built to the westward of this fosse. These particulars might be executed at no very great expence; but, I apprehend, they would be ineffectual, as the town is commanded by every hill in the neighbourhood; and the exhalations from stagnating sea-water would infallibly render the air unwholesome. Notwithstanding the undoubted antiquity of Nice, very few monuments of that antiquity now remain. The inhabitants say, they were either destroyed by the Saracens in their successive descents upon the coast, by the barbarous nations in their repeated incursions, or used in fortifying the castle, as well as in building other edifices. The city of Cemenelion, however, was subject to the same disasters, and even entirely ruined; nevertheless, we still find remains of its ancient splendor. There have been likewise a few stones found at Nice, with ancient inscriptions; but there is nothing of this kind standing, unless we give the name of antiquity to a marble cross on the road to Provence, about half a mile from the city. It stands upon a pretty high pedestal with steps, under a pretty stone cupola or dome, supported by four Ionic pillars, on the spot where Charles V. emperor of Germany, Francis I. of France, and pope Paul II. agreed to have a conference, in order to determine all their disputes. Th

LETTER XVII.

emperor came hither by sea, with a powerful fleet, and the French king by land, at the head of a numerous army. All the endeavours of his holiness, however, could not effect a peace; but they agreed to a truce of ten years. Mezerai affirms, that these two great princes never saw one another on this occasion; and that this shyness was owing to the management of the pope, whose private designs might have been frustrated had they come to a personal interview. In the front of the colonade, there is a small stone, with an inscription in Latin, which is so high, and so much defaced, that I cannot read it.

In the sixteenth century there was a college erected at Nice, by Emanuel Philibert, duke of Savoy, for granting degrees to students of law; and in the year one thousand six hundred and fourteen, Charles Emanuel I. instituted the senate of Nice; consisting of a president, and a certain number of senators, who are distinguished by their purple robes, and other ensigns of authority. They administer justice, having the power of life and death, not only thro' the whole county of Nice, but causes are evoked from Oneglia, and some other places, to their tribunal, which is the *dernier resort*, from whence there is no appeal. The commandant, however, by virtue of his military power and unrestricted authority, takes upon him to punish individuals by imprisonment, corporal pains, and banishment, without consulting the senate, or indeed observing any form of trial. The only redress against any unjust exercise of this absolute power, is by complaint to the king; and you know what chance a poor man has for being redressed in this manner.

With respect to religion, I may safely say, that here superstition reigns under the darkest shades of ignorance and prejudice. I think there are ten convents and three nunneries within and without the walls of Nice; and among them all, I never could hear of one man who had made any tolerable advances in any kind of human learning. All ecclesiastics are exempted from any exertion of civil power, being under the immediate protection and authority of the bishop, or his vicar. The bishop of Nice is suffragan of the archbishop of Ambrun in France; and the revenues of the see amount to between five and six hundred pounds sterling. We have likewise an office of the inquisition, though I do not hear that it presumes to execute any acts of jurisdiction, without the king's special permission. All the churches are sanctuaries for all kinds of criminals, except those guilty of high treason; and the priests are extremely jealous of their privileges in this particular. They receive, with open arms, murderers, robbers, smugglers, fradulent, bankrupts, and felons of every denomination; and never give them up, until after having stipulated for their lives and liberty. I need not enlarge upon the pernicious consequences of this infamous prerogative, calculated to ruse and extend the power and influence of the Roman church on the ruins of morality and good order. I saw a fellow, who had three days before murdered his wife in the last month of pregnancy, taking the air, with great composure and serenity, on the steps of a church in Florence; and nothing is more common, than to see the most execrable villans diverting themselves in the cloysters of some convents at Rome.

Nice abounds with noblesse, marquisses, counts, and barons. Of these, three or four families are really respectable the rest are *novi homines*, sprung from Bourgeois, who have saved a little money by their different occupations, and raised themselves to the rank of noblesse by purchase. One is descended from an avocat; another from an apothecary; a third from a retailer of wine; a fourth from a dealer in anchovies. and I am told, there is actually a count at Ville-franche, whose father sold macaroni in the streets. A man in this country may buy a marquisate, or a county, for the value of three or four hundred pounds sterling, and the title follows the fief: but he may purchase *lettres de nobleſſe* for about thirty or forty guineas. In Savoy there are six hundred families of nobleſſe; the greater part of which have not above one hundred crowns a year to maintain their dignity. In the mountains of Piedmont, and even in this county of Nice, there are some representatives of very antient and noble families reduced to the condition of common peasants; but they still retain the antient pride of their houses, and boast of the noble blood that runs in their veins. A gentleman told me, that in travelling through the mountains, he was obliged to pass a night in the cottage of one of these rusticated nobles, who called to his son in the evening, "*Chevalier, as tu donné a manger aux cochons.*" This, however, is not the case with the Nobleſſe of Nice. Two or three of them have about four or five hundred a year: the rest, in general may have about one hundred pistoles, arising from the silk, oil, wine, and oranges produced in their small plantations, where they have also country houses. Some few of these are well built, commodious, and agreeably situated; but, for the most part they are miserable enough. Our nobleſſe notwithstanding their origin, and the cheap rate at which their titles have been obtained, are nevertheleſs extremely tenacio[us] of their privileges, very delicate in maintaining the *etiquette*, and keep at a very stately distance from the Bourgeoise. How they live in their families, I do not chuse to inquire; but, in public, Madame appears in her robe of gold, or silver stuff, with her powder and friture, her perfumes, her paint and her patches; while Monsieur le Comte struts about in his lace and embroidery. Rouge and fard are more peculiarly necessary in this country, where the complexion and skin are naturally swarthy and yellow. I have likewise observed, that most of the females are pot-bellied; a circumstance owing, I believe, to the great quantity of vegetable trash which they eat. All the horses, mules, asses, and cattle, which feed upon grass, have the same distension. This kind of food produces such acid juices in the stomach, as excite a perpetual sense of hunger. I have been often amazed at the voracious appetites of these people. You must not expect that I should describe the tables and the hospitality of our Nissard gentry. Our consul, who is a very honest man, told me, he had lived four and thirty years in the country without having once eat or drank in any of their houses.

The noblesse of Nice cannot leave the country without express leave from the king; and this leave, when obtained, is for a limited time, which they dare not exceed, on pain of incurring his majesty's displeasure. They must, therefore, endeavour to find amusements at home; and this, I apprehend, would be no easy task for people of an active spirit or restless disposition. True it is, the religion of the country supplies a never-failing fund of pastime to those who have any relish for devotion, and this is here a prevailing taste. We have had transient visits of a puppet-shew, strolling musicians, and rope-dancers; but they did not like their quarters, and decamped without beat of drum. In the summer, about eight or nine at night, part of the noblesse may be seen assembled in a place called *the Parc*; which is, indeed, a sort of a street formed by a row of very paltry houses on one side, and on the other, by part of the town-wall, which screens it from a prospect of the sea, the only object that could render it agreeable. Here you may perceive the noblesse stretched in pairs upon logs of wood, like so many seals upon the rocks by moon-light, each dame with her *cicisbeo*: for you must understand this Italian fashion prevails at Nice among all ranks of people; and there is not such a passion as jealousy known. The husband and the *cicisbeo* live together as sworn brothers; and the wife and the mistress embrace each other with marks of warmth

LETTER XVII.

affection. I do not chuse to enter into particulars. I cannot open the scandalous chronicle of Nice, without hazard of contamination. With respect to delicacy and decorum, you may peruse Dean Swift's description of the Yahoos, and then you will have some idea of the *sporceerie* that distinguishes the gallantry of Nice. But the Parc is not the only place of public resort for our noblesse in a summer's evening. Just without one of our gates, you will find them seated in ditches on the highway side, serenaded with the croaking of frogs, and the bells and braying of mules and asses continually passing in a perpetual cloud of dust. Besides these amusements, there is a public *conversazione* every evening at the commandant's house called the *Government*, where those noble personages play at cards for farthings. In carnival time, there is also, at this same Government, a ball twice or thrice a week, carried on by subscription. At this assembly every person, without distinction, is permitted to dance in masquerade: but, after dancing, they are obliged to unmask, and if Bourgeois, to retire. No individual can give a ball, without obtaining a permission and guard of the commandant; and then his house is open to all masques, without distinction, who are provided with tickets, which tickets are sold by the commandant's secretary, at five sols a-piece, and delivered to the guard at the door. If I have a mind to entertain my particular friends, I cannot have more than a couple of violins; and, in that case, it is called a *conversazione*.

Though the king of Sardinia takes all opportunities to distinguish the subjects of Great-Britain with particular marks of respect, I have seen enough to be convinced that our nation is looked upon with an evil eye by the people of Nice; and this arises partly from religious prejudices, and partly from envy, occasioned by a ridiculous notion of our superior wealth. For my own part, I owe them nothing on the score of civilities; and therefore I shall say nothing more on the subject, lest I should be tempted to deviate from that temperance and impartiality which I would fain hope have hitherto characterised the remarks of,

 Dear Sir,

  Your faithful humble servant.

LETTER XVIII.

Nice, May 2, 1764.

DEAR DOCTOR,

I Wrote in May to Mr B—— at Geneva, and gave him what information he de-

LETTER XVIII.

fired to have, touching the conveniencies of Nice. I shall now enter into the same detail, for the benefit of such of your friends or patients as may have occasion to try this climate.

The journey from Calais to Nice, of four persons in a coach, or two post-chaises, with a servant on horseback, travelling post, may be performed with ease, for about one hundred and twenty pounds, including every expence. Either at Calais or at Paris, you will always find a travelling coach or berline, which you may buy for thirty or forty guineas, and this will serve very well to reconvey you to your own country.

In the town of Nice, you will find no ready furnished lodgings for a whole family. Just without one of the gates, there are two houses to be let, ready furnished, for about five loui'dores per month. As for the country houses in this neighbourhood, they are damp in winter, and generally without chimnies; and in summer they are rendered uninhabitable by the heat and the vermin. If you hire a tenement in Nice, you must take it for a year certain; and this will cost you about twenty pounds sterling. For this price, I have a ground floor paved with brick, consisting of a kitchen, two large halls, a couple of good rooms with chimnies, three large closets, that serve for bed-chambers and dreſſing rooms, a butler's room, and three apartments for ſervants lumber or ſtores, to which we aſcend by narrow wooden ſtairs. I have likewiſe two ſmall gardens, well ſtocked with oranges, lemons, peaches, figs, grapes, corinths, ſallad, and pot-herbs. It is ſupplied with a draw-well of good water, and there is another in the veſtibule of the houſe, which is cool, large, and magnificent. You may hire furniture for ſuch a tenement, for about two guineas a month, but I choſe rather to buy what was neceſſary; and this coſt me about ſixty pounds. I ſuppoſe it will fetch me about half the money when I leave the place. It is very difficult to find a tolerable cook at Nice. A common maid, who ſerves the people of the country for three or four livres a-month, will not live with an Engliſh family under eight or ten. They are all ſlovenly, ſlothful, and unconſcionable cheats. The markets at Nice are tollerably well ſupplied. Their beef, which comes from Piedmont, is pretty good, and we have it all the year. In the winter, we have likewiſe excellent pork, and delicate lamb but the mutton is indifferent. Piedmont alſo, affords us delicious capons, fed with Maiz; and this country produces excellent turkeys, but very few geeſe. Chickens and pullets are extremely meagre

I have tried to fatten them without success. In summer they are subject to the pip, and die in great numbers. Autumn and winter are the seasons for game; hares, partridges, quails, wild-pidgeons, woodcocks, snipes, thrushes, beccaficas, and ortolans. Wild-boar is sometimes found in the mountains: it has a delicious taste, not unlike that of the wild-hog in Jamaica; and would make an excellent barbecue, about the beginning of winter, when it is in good case: but, when meagre, the head only is presented at tables. Pheasants are very scarce. As for the heath-game, I never saw but one cock, which my servant bought in the market, and brought home, but the commandant's cook came into my kitchen, and carried it off, after it was half-plucked, saying, his master had company to dinner. The hares are large, plump, and juicy. The partridges are generally of the red sort; large as pullets, and of a good flavour. there are also some grey partridges in the mountains; and another sort, of a white colour, that weigh four or five pounds each. Beccaficas are smaller than sparrows, but very fat, and they are generally eat half raw. The best way of dressing them, is to stuff them into a roll, scooped of its crum; to baste them well with butter, and roast them untill they are brown and crisp. The ortolans are kept in cages, and crammed until they die of fat, then eaten as dainties. The thrush is presented with the trail, because the bird feeds on olives. They may as well eat the trail of a sheep, because it feeds on the aromatic herbs of the mountain. In the summer, we have beef, veal, mutton, chicken, and ducks; which last are very fat, and very flabby. All the meat is tough in this season, because the excessive heat, and great number of flies, will not admit of its being kept any time after it is killed. Butter and milk, though not very delicate, we have all the year. Our tea and fine sugar come from Marseilles, at a very reasonable price.

Nice is not without variety of fish; though they are not counted so good in their kind as those of the ocean. Soals and flat-fish, in general, are scarce. Here are some mullets, both greay and red. We sometimes see the dory, which is called *St Pietro;* with rock-fish, bonita, and mackarel. The gurnard appears pretty often; and there is plenty of a kind of large whiting, which eats pretty well, but has not the delicacy of that which is caught on our coast. One of the best fish of the country, is called *Le Loup,* about two or three pounds in weight; white, firm, and well-flavoured. Another, no way infe-

LETTER XVIII.

not to it, is the *Mouſtel*, about the ſame ſize, of a dark grey colour, and ſhort, blunt ſnout; growing thinner and flatter from the ſhoulders downwards, ſo as to reſemble a ſoal at the tail. This cannot be the *muſtula* of the Ancients, which is ſuppoſed to be the ſea-lamprey. Here too are found the *vyvre*, or, as we call it, *weaver;* remarkable for its long, ſharp ſpines, ſo dangerous to the fingers of the fiſhermen. We have abundance of the *ſepe*, or cuttle-fiſh, of which the people in this country make a delicate ragout; as alſo of the *polype de mer*, which is an ugly animal, with long feelers, like tails, which they often wind about the legs of the fiſhermen. They are ſtewed with onions, and eat ſomething like cow heel. The market ſometimes affords the *ecrviſſe de mer*, which is a lobſter without claws, of a ſweetiſh taſte, and there are a few rock-oyſters, very ſmall and very rank. Sometimes the fiſhermen find under water pieces of a very hard cement, like plaiſter of Paris, which contain a kind of muſcle, called *la datte*, from its reſemblance to a date. Theſe petrefactions are commonly of a triangular form, and may weigh about about twelve or fifteen pounds each; and one of them may contain a dozen of theſe muſcles, which have nothing extraordinary in the taſte or flavour, tho' extremely curious, as found alive and juicy in the heart of a rock, almost as hard as marble, without any visible communication with the air or water. I take it for granted, however, that the inclosing cement is porous, and admits the finer parts of the surrounding fluid. In order to reach the muscles, this cement must be broke with large hammers; and it may be truly said, the kernel is not worth the trouble of cracking the shell. Among the fish of this country, there is a very ugly animal of the eel species, which might pass for a serpent: it is of a dusky, black colour, marked with spots of yellow, about eighteen inches, or two feet long. The Italians call it *murena*, but whether it is the fish which had the same name among the ancient Romans, I cannot pretend to determine. The ancient murena was counted a great delicacy, and was kept in ponds for extraordinary occasions. Julius Cæsar borrowed six thousand for one entertainment: but I imagined this was the river lamprey. The murena of this country is in no esteem, and only eaten by the poor people. Craw-fish and trout are rarely found in the rivers among the mountains. The sword-fish is much esteemed in Nice, and called *l'empereur*, about six or seven feet long: but I have never seen it †.

† Since I wrote the above letter, I have eaten

They are very scarce; and, when taken, are generally concealed, because the head belongs to the commandant, who has likewise the privilege of buying the best fish at a very low price. For which reason, the choice pieces are concealed by the fishermen, and sent privately to Piedmont or Genoa. But, the chief fisheries on this coast, are of the sardines, anchovies, and tunny. These are taken in small quantities all the year; but spring and summer is the season when they mostly abound. In June and July, a fleet of about fifty fishing boats puts to sea every evening about eight o'clock, and catch anchovies in immense quantities. One small boat sometimes takes in one night twenty-five rup, amounting to six hundred weight; but it must be observed, that the pound here, as well as in other parts of Italy, consists but of twelve ounces. Anchovies, besides their making considerable article in the commerce of Nice, are a great resource in all families. The noblesse and bourgeois sup on sallad and anchovies, which are eaten on all their meagre days. The fishermen and mariners all along this coast have scarce any other food but dry bread, with a few

several times of this fish, which is as white as the finest veal, and extremely delicate. The emperor associates with the tunny fish, and is always taken in their company.

pickled anchovies; and when the fish is eaten, they rub their crusts with the brine. Nothing can be more delicious than fresh anchovies fried in oil. I prefer them to the smelts of the Thames. I need not mention, that the sardines and anchovies are caught in nets; salted, barrelled, and exported into all the different kingdoms and states of Europe. The sardines, however, are largest and fattest in the month of September. A company of adventurers have farmed the tunny-fishery of the king, for six years; a monopoly for which they pay about three thousand pounds sterling. They are at a considerable expence for nets, boats, and attendance. Their nets are disposed in a very curious manner across the small bay of Carpice, in this neighbourhood, where the fish chiefly resort. They are never removed, except in the winter, and when they want repair: but there are avenues for the fish to enter, and pass from one inclosure to another. There is a man in a boat, who constantly keeps watch. When he perceives they are fairly entered, he has a method for shutting all the passes, and confining the fish to one apartment of the net, which is lifted up into the boat until the prisoners are taken and secured. The tunny fish generally runs from fifty to one hundred weight; but some of them are much larger. They are immediately gutted, boiled, and cut in flices. The guts and head afford oil: the flices are partly dried, to be eaten occafionally with oil and vinegar, or barrelled up in oil, to be exported. It is counted a delicacy in Italy and Piedmont, and taftes not unlike fturgeon. The famous pickle of the Ancients, called *garum*, was made of the gills and blood of the tunny, or thynnus. There is a much more confiderable fifhery of it in Sardinia, where it is faid to employ four hundred perfons; but this belongs to the duc de St Pierre. In the neighbourhood of Villa-franca, there are people always employed in fifhing for coral and fponge, which grow adhering to the rocks under water. Their methods do not favour much of ingenuity. For the coral, they lower down a fwab, compofed of what is called *punyarn* on board our fhips of war, hanging in diftinct threads, and funk by means of a great weight, which ftriking againft the coral in its defcent, difengages it from the rocks; and fome of the pieces being entangled among the threads of the fwab, are brought up with it above water. The fponge is got by means of a crofs-ftick, fitted with hooks, which being lowered down, faftens upon it, and tears it from the rocks. In fome parts of the Adriatic and Archipelago, these substances are gathered by divers, who can remain five mintues below water. But I will not detain you one minute longer; though I must observe, that there is plenty of fine samphire growing along all these rocks, neglected and unknown. Adieu.

LETTER XIX.

Nice, October 10 : 64

DEAR SIR,

BEFORE I tell you the price of provisions at Nice, it will be necessary to say something of the money. The gold coin of Sardinia consists of the doppia di Savoia, value twenty-four livres Piemontese, about the size of a lou'dore; and the mezzo doppia, or piece of twelve livres. In silver, there is the scudo of six livres, the mezzo scudo of three; and the quarto, or pezza di trenta soldi; but all these are very scarce. We seldom see any gold and silver coin, but the lou'dore, and the six, and three livre pieces of France; sure sign that the French suffer by the contraband commerce with the Island. The coin chiefly used at market is that of copper silvered, that passes for six fols and a half; another of the fame fort, value two fols and a half. They have on one fide the impreffion of the king's head; and on the other, the arms of Savoy, with a ducal crown, infcribed with his name and titles. There are of genuine copper, pieces of one fol, ftamped on one fide with a crofs fleuree; and on the reverfe, with the king's cypher and crown, infcribed as the others: finally, there is another fmall copper piece, called *piccalon*, the fixth part of a fol, with a plain crofs, and on the reverfe a flip knot furmounted with a crown, the legend as above. The impreffion and legend on the gold and filver coins, are the fame as thofe on the pieces of feven fols and a half. The livre of Piedmont confifts of twenty fols, and is very near of the fame value as an Englifh fhilling: ten fols, therefore, are equal to fix-pence fterling. Butcher's meat in general fells at Nice for three fols a pound; and veal is fomething dearer. but then there are but twelve ounces in the pound, which being allowed for, fifteen ounces come for fomething lefs than twopence halfpenny Englifh. Fifh commonly fells for four fols the twelve ounces, or five for the Englifh pound; and thefe five are equivalent to three-pence of our money. but fometimes we are obliged to pay five, and even fix fols for the Piedmontese pound of fish. A turkey that would sell for five or six shillings at the London market, costs me but thrice at Nice. I can buy a good capon for thirty sols, or eighteen-pence; and the same price I pay for a brace of partridges, or a good hare. I can have a woodcock for twenty-four sols; but the pidgeons are dearer than in London. Rabbits are very rare, and there is scarce a goose to be seen in the whole county of Nice. Wild-ducks and teal are sometimes to be had in the winter. And now I am speaking of sea-fowl, it may not be amiss to tell you what I know of the halcyon, or king's fisher. It is a bird, though very rare in this country, about the size of a pigeon; the body brown, and the belly white by a wonderful instinct, it makes its nest upon the surface of the sea, and lays its eggs in the month of November, when the Mediterranean is always calm and smooth as a mill-pond. The people here call them *martinets*, because they begin to hatch about Martinmas. Their nests are sometimes seen floating near the shore, and generally become the prize of the boys, who are very alert in catching them.

You know all sea-birds are allowed by the church of Rome to be eaten on meagre days, as a kind of fish; and the monks especially do not fail to make use of the permission. Sea turtle, or tortoises, are often found at sea by the mariners, in these latitudes: but they are not the green sort, so much in request among the aldermen of London. All the Mediterranean turtle are of the kind called *loggerhead*, which in the West-Indies are eaten by none but hungry seamen, negroes, and the lowest class of people. One of these, weighing about two hundred pounds, was lately brought on shore by the fishermen of Nice, who found it floating asleep on the surface of the sea. The whole town was alarmed at sight of such a monster, the nature of which they could not comprehend. However, the monks called *Minims*, of St Francisco di Paolo, guided by a sure instinct, marked it as their prey, and surrounded it accordingly. The friars of other convents, not quite so hungry, crowding down to the beach, declared it should not be eaten, dropped some hints about the possibility of its being præternatural and diabolical, and even proposed exorcisms and aspersions with holy water. The populace were divided according to their attachment to this or that convent: a mighty clamour arose; and the police, in order to remove the cause of their contention, ordered the tortoise to be re-committed to the waves; a sentence which the Franciscans saw executed, not without sighs and lamentation. The land turtle, or terrapin, is much better known at Nice, as being a native of this county; yet the best are brought from the island of Sardinia. The soup or *bouillon* of this animal is always prescribed here as a great restorative to consumptive patients. The bread of Nice is very indifferent, and I am persuaded very unwholsome. The flour is generally musty, and not quite free of sand. This is either owing to the particles of the mill-stone rubbed off in grinding, or to what adheres to the corn itself, in being threshed upon the common ground; for there are no threshing-floors in this country. I shall now take notice of the vegetables of Nice. In the winter, we have green pease, asparagus, artichoaks, cauliflower, beans, French beans, celery; and endive, cabbage, coleworts, radishes, turnips, carrots, betueraves, sorrel, lettuce, onions, garlic, and chalot. We have potatoes from the mountains, mushrooms, champignoms, and truffles. Piedmont affords white truffles, counted the most delicious in the world: they sell for about three livres the pound. The fruits of this season, are pickled olives, oranges, lemons, citrons, citronelles, dried figs, grapes, apples, pears, almonds, chesnuts, walnuts, filberts, medlars, pomegranates, and a fruit called azerolles, about the size of a nutmeg, of an oblong shape, red colour, and agreeable acid taste. I might likewise add the cherry of the *laurus cerasus*, which is sold in the market; very beautiful to the eye, but insipid to the palate. In summer we have all those vegetables in perfection. There is also a kind of small scourge, or gourd, of which the people of the country make a very savoury ragout, with the help of eggs, cheese, and fresh anchovies. Another is made of the badenjean, which the Spaniards call *berengena*: it is much eaten in Spain and the Levant, as well as by the Moors in Barbary. It is about the size and shape of a hen's egg, inclosed in a cup like an acorn; when ripe, of a faint purple colour. It grows on a stalk about a foot high, with long spines or prickles. The people here have different ways of slicing and dressing it, by broiling, boiling, and stewing, with other ingredients: but it is at best an insipid dish. There are some caper-bushes in this neighbourhood, which grow wild in holes of garden walls, and require no sort of cultivation: in one or two gardens, there are palm-trees; but the dates never open. In my register of the weather, I have marked the seasons of the principal fruits in this country. In May we have straw-berries, which continue in season two or three months; these are of the wood kind, very grateful, and of a good flavour; but the scarlets and hautboys are not known at Nice. In the beginning of June, and even sooner, the cherries begin to be ripe. They are a kind of bleeding hearts; large, fleshy, and high flavoured, though rather too luscious. I have likewise seen a few of those we call Kentish cherries, which are much more cool, acid, and agreeable, especially in this hot climate. The cherries are succeeded by the apricots and peaches, which are all standards, and of consequence better flavoured than what we call wall-fruit. The trees, as well as almonds, grow and bear without care and cultivation, and may be seen in the open fields about Nice: but without proper culture the fruit degenerates. The best peaches I have seen at Nice are the almberges, of a yellow hue, and oblong shape, about the size of a small lemon. Their consistence is much more solid than that of our English peaches, and their taste more delicious. Several trees of this kind I have in my own garden. Here is likewise plenty of other sorts; but no nectarines. We have little choice of plumbs. Neither do I admire the pears and apples of this country but the most aggreeable apples I ever tasted come from Final, and are called *pom.i carli*

The greatest fault I find with most fruits in this climate is, that they are too sweet and luscious, and want that agreeable acid which is so cooling and so grateful in a hot country. This, too, is the case with our grapes, of which there is great plenty and variety, plump and juicy, and large as plumbs. Nature, however, has not neglected to provide other agreeable vegetable juices to cool the human body. During the whole summer we have plenty of musk-melons. I can buy one as large as my head for the value of one English penny: but one of the best and largest, weighing ten or twelve pounds, I can have for twelve sols, or about eight-pence sterling. From Antibes and Sardinia we have another fruit, called a water-melon, which is well known in Jamaica, and some of our other colonies. Those from Antibes are about the size of an ordinary bomb-shell: but the Sardinian and Jamaica water-melons are four times as large. The skin is green, smooth, and thin. The inside is a purple pulp, studded with broad, flat, black seeds, and impregnated with a juice the most cool, delicate and refreshing, that can well be conceived. One would imagine the pulp itself dissolved in the stomach; for you may eat of it until you are filled up to the tongue, without feeling the least inconvenience. It is so friendly to the constitution, that in ardent inflammatory fevers, it is drank as the best emulsion. At Genoa, Florence, and Rome, it is sold in the streets, ready cut in slices, and the porters, sweating under their burdens, buy and eat them as they pass. A porter of London quenches his thirst with a draught of strong beer: a porter of Rome, or Naples, refreshes himself with a slice of water-melon, or a glass of iced-water. The one costs three half-pence, the last, half a farthing—which of them is most effectual? I am sure the men are equally pleased. It is commonly remarked, that beer strengthens as well as refreshes. But the porters of Constantinople, who never drink any thing stronger than water, and eat very little animal food, will lift and carry heavier burdens than any other porters in the known world. If we may believe the most respectable travellers, a Turk will carry a load of seven hundred weight, which is more (I believe) than any English porter ever attempted to raise.

Among the refreshments of these warm countries, I ought not to forget mentioning the sorbettes, which are sold in coffee houses, and places of public resort. They are iced froth, made with juice of oranges, apricots, or peaches; very agreeable to the palate, and so extremely cold, that I was afraid to swallow them in this h country, until I found, from information and experience, that they may be taken in moderation, without any bad confequence.

Another confiderable article in houfekeeping is wine, which we have here good and reafonable. The wine of Tavelle in Languedoc is very near as good as Burgundy, and may be had at Nice at the rate of fixpence a bottle. The fweet wine of St Laurent, counted equal to that of Frontignan, cofts about eight or ninepence a quart: pretty good Malaga may be had for half the money. Thofe who make their own wine, chufe the grapes from different vineyards, and have them picked, preffed, and fermented at home. That which is made by the peafants, both red and white, is generally genuine: but the wine merchants of Nice brew and balderdafh, and even mix it with pigeons dung and quick-lime. It cannot be fuppofed that a ftranger and fojourner fhould buy his own grapes, and make his own provifion of wine: but he may buy it by recommendation from the peafants, for about eighteen or twenty livres the charge, confifting of eleven up five pounds; in other words, of two hundred and eighty pounds of his country, fo as to bring it to fomething lefs than three-pence a quart. The Nice wine, when mixed with water, makes an agreeable beverage. There is an inferior fort for servants, drank by the common people, which in the cabaret does not cost above a penny a bottle. The people here are not so nice as the English, in the management of their wine. It is kept in flacons, or large flasks, without corks, having a little oil at top. It is not deemed the worse for having been opened a day or two before; and they expose it to the hot sun, and all kinds of weather, without hesitation. Certain it is, this treatment has little or no effect upon its taste, flavour, and transparency.

The brandy of Nice is very indifferent; and the *liqueurs* are so sweetened with coarse sugar, that they scarce retain the taste or flavour of any other ingredient.

The last article of domestic œconomy which I shall mention is fuel, or wood for firing, which I buy for eleven sols (a little more than six-pence halfpenny) a quintal, consisting of one hundred and fifty-pound Nice weight. The best, which is of oak, comes from Sardinia. The common sort is olive, which being cut with the sap in it, ought to be laid in during the summer; otherwise, it will make a very uncomfortable fire. In my kitchen and two chambers, I burned fifteen thousand weight of wood in four weeks, exclusive of charcoal for the kitchen stoves and of pine tops for lighting the fires

LETTER XIX.

These last are as large as pine-apples, which they greatly resemble in shape, and to which indeed they give their name; and being full of turpentine, make a wonderful blaze. For the same purpose, the people of these countries use the *farments*, or cuttings of the vines, which they sell made up in small fascines. This great consumption of wood is owing to the large fires used in rosting pieces of beef, and joints, in the English manner. The roasts of this country seldom exceed two or three pounds of meat; and then other *plats* are made over stove-holes. But it is now high time to conduct you from the kitchen, where you have been too long detained by

Your humble servant.

P. S. I have mentioned the prices of almost all the articles in house-keeping, as they are paid by the English: but, exclusive of butcher's meat, I am certain the natives do not pay so much by thirty per cent. Their imposition on us, is not only a proof of their own villainy and hatred, but a scandal on their government; which ought to interfere in favour of the subjects of a nation to which they are so much bound in point of policy as well as gratitude.

LETTER XX.

Nice, October 22. 1764.

DEAR SIR,

AS I have nothing else to do but to satisfy my own curiosity, and that of my friends, I obey your injunctions with pleasure; though not without some apprehension that my inquiries will afford you very little entertainment. The place where I am is of very little importance or consequence as a state or community; neither is there any thing curious or interesting in the character or œconomy of its inhabitatnts.

There are some few merchants in Nice, said to be in good circumstances. I know one of them, who deals to a considerable extent, and goes twice a year to London to attend the sales of the East-India company. He buys up a very large quantity of muslins, and other India goods, and freights a ship in the river to transport them to Villa-franca. Some of these are sent to Swisserland; but, I believe, the greater part is smuggled into France by virtue of counterfeit stamps, which are here used without any ceremony. Indeed, the chief commerce of this place is a contraband traffic carried on to the disadvantage of France; and I am told that the farmers of the Levant company in that kingdom find their account in conniving at it. Certain it is, a great quantity of merchandize is brought hither every week by mules from Turin and other parts in Piedmont, and afterwards conveyed to the other side of the Var, either by land or water. The mules of Piedmont are exceeding strong and hardy. One of them will carry a burden of near six hundred weight. They are easily nourished, and require no other respite from their labour but the night's repose. They are the only carriage that can be used in crossing the mountains, being very sure-footed: and it is observed, that in chusing their steps, they always march upon the brink of the precipice. You must let them take their own way, otherwise you will be in danger of losing your life; for they are obstinate, even to desperation. It is very dangerous to meet those animals on horseback: they have such an aversion to horses, that they will attack them with incredible fury, so as even to tear them and their riders in pieces; and the best method for avoiding this fate, is to clap spurs to your beast, and seek your safety in flight. I have been more than once obliged to fly before them. They always give you warning, by raising a hideous braying as soon as they perceive the horse at a distance. The mules of Provence are not so mischievous, because they are more used to the sight and society of horses. but those of Piedmont are by far the largest and the strongest I have seen.

Some very feasible schemes for improving the commerce of Nice have been presented to the ministry of Turin; but hitherto without success. The English import annually between two and three thousand bales of raw silk, the growth of Piedmont; and this is embarked either at Genoa or Leghorn. We likewise take a considerable quantity of fruit and oil at Oneglia, St Remo, and other places in this neighbourhood. All these commodities might be embarked at a smaller expence at Nice, which is a free port, where no duties are paid by the exporter. Besides, the county of Nice itself produces a considerable quantity of hemp, oranges, lemons, and very good oil and anchovies, with some silk and wine, which last is better than that of Languedoc, and far excels the port drank in England. This wine is of a strong body, a good flavour, keeps very well, and improves by sea-carriage. I am told that some of the wine-merchants here transport French wine from Languedoc and Provence, and enter it in England as the produce of

Nice or Italy. If the merchants of Nice would establish magazines of raw silk, oil, wine, &c. at Nice, and their correspondents at London send hither ships at stated periods, laden with India goods, hard-ware, and other manufactures of England, which would find a vent in this country, in Piedmont, Savoy, Swisserland, and Provence, then the commerce of this town would flourish, more especially if the king would lay out the necessary expence for rendering the harbour more commodious and secure. But this is not a matter of very great consequence, as there is an excellent harbour at Ville-franche, which is not more than a mile and a half from that of Nice. But the great objection to the improvement of commerce at Nice, is the want of money, industry, and character. The natives themselves are in general such dirty knaves, that no foreigners will trust them in the way of trade. They have been known to fill their oil-casks half full of water, and their anchovy-barrels with stinking heads of that fish, in order to cheat their correspondents.

The shopkeepers of this place are generally poor, greedy, and over-reaching. Many of them are bankrupts of Marseilles, Genoa, and other countries, who have fled from their creditors to Nice; which, being a free port, affords an asylum to foreign cheats and sharpers of every denomination. Here is likewise a pretty confiderable number of Jews, who live together in a street appropriated for their use, which is shut up every night. They act as brokers; but are generally poor, and deal in frippery, remnants, old cloaths, and old houshold furniture. There is another branch of traffic engroffed by the monks. Some convents have such a number of masses bequeathed to them, that they find it impossible to execute the will of the donors. In this case, they agree by the lump with the friars of poorer convents, who say the masses for less money than has been allowed by the defunct, and their employers pocket the difference: for example, my grandfather bequeaths a sum of money to a certain convent, to have such a number of masses said for the repose of his soul, at the price of ten sols each, and this convent, not having time to perform them, bargains with the friars of another to say them for six sols a-piece, so that they gain four sols upon every mass; for it matters not to the soul of the deceased where they are said, so they be properly authenticated. A poor gentleman of Nice, who piques himself much on the noble blood that runs in his veins, though he has not a pair of whole breeches to wear, complained to me, that his great grandmother had founded a perpetual mass for the repose of her own soul, at the rate of fifteen sols (nine pence English) a day; which indeed was all that now remained of the family estate. He said, what made the hardship the greater on him, she had been dead above fifty years, and in all probability her soul had got out of purgatory long ago; therefore the continuance of the mass was an unnecessary expence. I told him, I thought in such a case the defunct should appear before the civil magistrate, and make affidavit of her being at peace, for the advantage of the family. He mused a little, and shrugging up his shoulders, replied, that where the interest of the church was at stake, he did not believe a spirit's declaration would be held legal evidence. In some parts of France, the curè of the parish, on All Soul's day, which is called *le jour des morts*, says a *libera Domine* for two sols, at every grave in the burying ground, for the release of the soul whose body is there interred.

The artisans of Nice are very lazy, very needy, very aukward, and void of all ingenuity. The price of their labour is very near as high as at London or Paris. Rather than work for moderate profit, arising from constant employment, which would comfortably maintain them and their families, they chuse to starve at home, to lounge about the ramparts, bask themselves in the sun, or play at bowls in the streets from morning till night.

The lowest class of people consists of fishermen, day-labourers, porters, and peasants: these last are distributed chiefly in the small cassines in the neighbourhood of the city, and are said to amount to twelve thousand. They are employed in labouring the ground, and have all the outward signs of extreme misery. They are all diminutive, meagre, withered, dirty, and half naked; in their complections, not barely swarthy, but as black as Moors; and I believe, in my conscience, many of them are descendants of that people. They are very hard-favoured; and their women in general have the coarsest features I have ever seen: it must be owned, however, they have the finest teeth in the world. The nourishment of those poor creatures consists of the refuse of the garden, very coarse bread, a kind of meal called *polenta*, made of Indian corn, which is very nourishing and agreeable, and a little oil but even in these particulars they seem to be stinted to very scanty meals. I have known a peasant feed his family with the skins of boiled beans. Their hogs are much better fed than their children. 'Tis pity they have no cows, which would yield milk, butter, and cheese, for the sustenance of their families. With all this wretchedness, one of these peasants will not work in your garden for less than eighteen sols, about eleven pence sterling, *per diem*; and then he does not half the work of an English labourer. If there is fruit in it, or any thing he can convey, he will infallibly steel it, if you do not keep a very watchful eye over him. All the common people are thieves and beggars; and I believe this is always the case with people who are extremely indigent and miserable. In other respects, they are seldom guilty of excesses. They are remarkably respectful and submissive to their superiors. The populace of Nice are very quiet and orderly. They are little addicted to drunkenness. I have never heard of one not since I lived among them; and murder and robbery are altogether unknown. A man may walk alone over the county of Nice, at midnight, without danger of insult. The police is very well regulated. No man is permitted to wear a pistol or dagger, on pain of being sent to the gallies. I am informed, that both murder and robbery are very frequent in some parts of Piedmont. Even here, when the peasants quarrel in their cups, (which very seldom happens,) they draw their knives, and the one infallibly stabs the other. To such extremities, however, they never proceed, except when there is a woman

in the cafe; and mutual jealoufy co-ope-
rates with the liquor they have drank, to
inflame their paffions. In Nice, the common people retire to their lodgings at
eight o'clock in winter, and nine in fummer. Every perfon found in the ftreets
after thefe hours, is apprehended by the
patrole; and, if he cannot give a good
account of himfelf, fent to prifon. At
nine in winter, and ten in fummer, there
is a curfew-bell rung, warning the people
to put out their lights, and go to bed.
This is a very neceffary precaution in towns
fubject to conflagrations; but of fmall ufe
in Nice, where there is very little com-
buftible in the houfes.

The punifhments inflicted upon malefactors and delinquents at Nice are hanging
for capital crimes; flavery on board the
gallies for a limited term, or for life, according to the nature of the tranfgreffion;
flagellation, and the ftrappado. This laft
is performed, by hoifting up the criminal
by his hands tied behind his back, on a
pulley about two ftories high; from whence,
the rope being fuddenly flackened, he falls
to within a yard or two of the ground,
where he is ftopped with a violent fhock,
arifing from the weight of his body, and
the velocity of his defcent, which generally diflocates his fhoulders, with incredible pain. This dreadful execution

sometimes repeated in a few minutes on the same delinquent; so that the very ligaments are tore from his joints, and his arms are rendered useless for life.

The poverty of the people in this country, as well as in the South of France, may be conjectured from the appearance of their domestic animals. The draught-horses, mules, and asses of the peasants, are so meagre, as to excite compassion. There is not a dog to be seen in tolerable case; and the cats are so many emblems of famine, frightfully thin, and dangerously rapacious. I wonder the dogs and they do not devour young children. Another proof of that indigence which reigns among the common people is this: you may pass thro' the whole South of France, as well as the county of Nice, where there is no want of groves, woods, and plantations, without hearing the song of black-bird, thrush, linnet, gold-finch, or any other bird whatsoever. All is silent and solitary. The poor birds are destroyed, or driven for refuge into other countries, by the savage persecution of the people, who spare no pains to kill, and catch them for their own subsistence. Scarce a sparrow, red-breast, tom-tit, or wren, can 'scape the guns and snares of those indefatigable fowlers. Even the noblesse make parties to go *a la chasse;* that is, to kill those little birds, which they eat as *gibier*.

The great poverty of the people here is owing to their religion. Half of their time is lost in observing the great number of festivals; and half of their substance is given to mendicant friars and parish priests. But if the church occasions their indigence, it likewise, in some measure, alleviates the horrors of it, by amusing them with shews, processions, and even those very feasts, which afford a recess from labour, in a country where the climate disposes them to idleness. If the peasants in the neighbourhood of any chapel dedicated to a saint, whose day is to be celebrated, have a mind to make a *festin*, in other words, a fair, they apply to the commandant of Nice for a licence, which costs them about a French crown. This being obtained, they assemble after service, men and women, in their best apparel, and dance to the music of fiddles, and pipe and tabor, or rather pipe and drum. There are hucksters stands, with pedlary ware and knickknacks for presents; cakes and bread, *liqueurs* and wine; and thither generally resort all the company of Nice. I have seen our whole noblesse at one of these *festins*, kept on the highway in summer, mingled with an immense crowd of peasants, mules, and asses, covered with dust, and sweating at every pore with the excessive heat of the weather. I should be much puzzled to tell whence their enjoyment arises on such occasions; or to explain their motives for going thither, unless they are prescribed it for penance, as a fore-taste of purgatory.

Now I am speaking of religious institutions, I cannot help observing, that the antient Romans were still more superstitious than the modern Italians; and that the number of their religious feasts, sacrifices, fasts, and holidays, was even greater than those of the Christian church of Rome. They had their *festi* and *profesti*, their *feriæ stativæ*, and *conceptivæ*, their fixed and moveable feasts; their *esuriales*, or fasting days, and their *precidaneæ*, or vigils. The *agonales* were celebrated in January; the *carmentales* in January and February; the *lupercales* and *matronales* in March; the *floralio* in May; the *saturnalia, robigalia, venalia, vertumnalia, fornacalia, palilia,* and *laralia*. They had their *latinæ*, their *paganales*, their *sementinæ*, their *compitales*, and their *imperativæ*; such as the *novemdalia*, instituted by the senate, on account of a supposed shower of stones. Besides, every private family had a number of *feriæ*, kept either by way of rejoicing for some benefit, or mourning for some calamity. Every time it thundered, the day was kept holy. Every-ninth day was a holiday, thence called *nundinæ, quasi novendinæ.* There was the *dies denominalis,* which was the fourth of the kalends, nones and ides of every month; over and above, the anniversary of every great defeat which the republic had sustained, particularly the *dies alliensis,* or fifteenth of the kalends of December, on which the Romans were totally defeated by the Gauls and Veientes, as Lucan says—*et damnata diu Romanis allia fastis.* The vast variety of their deities, said to amount to thirty thousand, with their respective rites of adoration, could not fail to introduce such a number of ceremonies, shews, sacrifices, lustrations, and public processions, as must have employed the people almost constantly from one end of the year to the other. This continual dissipation must have been a great enemy to industry; and the people must have been idle and effeminate. I think it would be no difficult matter to prove, that there is very little difference, in point of character, between the antient and modern inhabitants of Rome; and that the great figure which this empire made of old, was not so much owing to the intrinsic virtue of its citizens, as to the barbarism, ignorance and imbecility of the nations they subdued. Instances of public and private virtue I find as frequent and as striking in the history of other nations, as in the annals of antient Rome; and now that the kingdoms and states of Europe are pretty equally enlightened, and ballanced in the scale of political power, I am of opinion, that if the most fortunate generals of the Roman common-wealth were again placed at the head of the very armies they once commanded, instead of extending their conquests over all Europe and Asia, they would hardly be able to subdue, and retain under their dominion, all the petty republics that subsist in Italy.

But I am tired with writing; and I believe you will be tired with reading this long letter, notwithstanding all your prepossession in favour of

Your very humble servant.

LETTER XXI.

Nice, November 10, 1764.

DEAR DOCTOR,

IN my inquiries about the revenues of Nice, I am obliged to trust to the information of the inhabitants, who are much given to exaggerate. They tell me the revenues of this town amount to one hundred thoufand livres, or five thoufand pounds fterling; of which I would ftrike off at leaft one fourth, as an addition of their own vanity perhaps, if we deduct a third, it will be nearer the truth. For I cannot find out any other funds they have, but the butchery and the bakery, which they farm at fo much a year to the beft bidder; and the *droits de entree*, or duties upon provifion brought into the city; but thefe are very fmall. The king is faid to draw from Nice one hundred thoufand livres annually, arifing from a free-gift, amounting to feven hundred pounds fterling, in lieu of the taille, from which this town and country are exempted; an inconfiderable duty upon wine fold in public-houfes; and the *droits du port*. Thefe laft confift of anchorage, paid by all veffels in proportion to their tonnage, when they enter the harbours of Nice and Villa-franca. Befides, all foreign veffels, under a certain ftipulated burden, that pafs between the ifland of Sardinia and this coaft, are obliged, in going to the eaftward, to enter and pay a certain regulated impofition, on pain of being taken and made prize. The prince of Monaco exacts a talliage of the fame kind; and both he and the king of Sardinia maintain armed cruifers to affert this prerogative; from which, however the Englifh and French are exempted by treaty, in consequence of having paid a sum of money at once. In all probability it was originally given as a consideration for maintaining lights on the shore, for the benefit of navigators, like the toll paid for passing the Sound in the Baltic. The fanal, or lanthorn, to the eastward of Villa-franca, is kept in good repair, and still lighted in the winter. The toll, however, is a very troublesome tax upon feluccas, and other small craft, which are greatly retarded in their voyages, and often lose the benefit of a fair wind, by being obliged to run in shore, and enter those harbours. The tobacco, which is mostly from the Levant, the king manufactures at his own expence, and sells for his own profit, at a very high price; and every person convicted of selling this commodity in secret, is sent to the gallies for life. The salt comes chiefly from Sardinia, and is stored up in the king's magazine; from whence it is exported to Piedmont, and other parts of his inland dominions. And here it may not be amiss to observe, that Sardinia produces very good horses, well-shaped, though small; strong, hardy, full of mettle, and easily fed. The whole county of Nice is said to yield the king half a million of livres, about twenty-five thousand pounds sterling, arising from a small donative made by every town and village: for the lands pay no tax or impofition, but the tithes to the church. His revenue then flows from the *gabelle* on falt and wine, and thefe free-gifts; fo that we may ftrike off one fifth of the fum at which the whole is eftimated; and conclude, that the king draws from the county of Nice, about four hundred thoufand livres, or twenty thoufand pounds fterling. That his revenues from Nice are not great, appears from the fmallnefs of the appointments allowed to his officers. The prefident has about three hundred pounds *per annum*, and the intendant about two. The pay of the commandant does not exceed three hundred and fifty pounds: but he has certain privileges called the *tour du baton*, fome of which a man of fpirit would not infift upon. He who commands at prefent, having no eftate of his own, enjoys a fmall commandery, which being added to his appointments at Nice, make the whole amount to about five hundred pounds fterling.

If we may believe the politicians of Nice, the king of Sardinia's whole revenue does not fall fhort of twenty millions of Piedmontefe livres, being about one million of our money. It muft be owned, that there is no country in Chriftendom lefs taxed than that of Nice; and as the foil produces the neceffaries of life, the inhabitants, with a little industry, might renew the golden age in this happy climate, among their groves, woods, and mountains, beautified with fountains, brooks, rivers, torrents, and cascades. In the midst of these pastoral advantages, the peasants are poor and miserable. They have no stock to begin the world with. They have no leases of the lands they cultivate; but entirely depend, from year to year, on the pleasure of the arbitrary land-holder, who may turn them out at a minute's warning, and they are oppressed by the mendicant friars and parish priests, who rob them of the best fruits of their labour. After all, the ground is too scanty for the number of families which are crouded on it.

You desire to know the state of the arts and sciences at Nice; which, indeed, is almost a total blank. I know not what men of talents this place may have formerly produced; but at present, it seems to be consecrated to the reign of dulness and superstition. It is very surprising to see a people established between two enlightened nations so devoid of taste and literature. Here are no tolerable pictures, busts, statues, nor edifices the very ornaments of the churches are wretchedly conceived, and worse executed. They have no public nor private libraries, that afford any thing worth perusing. There is not even a bookseller in Nice. Though they value themselves upon being natives of Italy, they are unacquainted with music. The few that play upon instruments, attend only to the execution. They have no genius nor taste, nor any knowledge of harmony and composition. Among the French, a Nissard piques himself on being Provencal; but in Florence, Milan, or Rome, he claims the honour of being born a native of Italy. The people of condition here speak both languages equally well; or, rather, equally ill, for they use a low, uncouth phraseology; and their pronunciation is extremely vitious. Their vernacular tongue is what they call *Patois*, though, in so calling it, they do it injustice.——*Patois*, from the Latin word *patavinitas*, means no more than a provincial accent or dialect. It takes its name from *Patavium*, or Padua, which was the birth-place of Livy; who, with all his merit as a writer, has admitted into his history some provincial expressions of his own country. The *Patois*, or native tongue of Nice, is no other than the ancient Provencal, from which the Italian, Spanish, and French languages have been formed. This is the language that rose upon the ruins of the Latin tongue, after the irruptions of the Goths, Vandals, Huns, and Burgundians, by whom the

Roman empire was destroyed. It was spoke all over Italy, Spain, and the southern parts of France, until the thirteenth century, when the Italians began to polish it into the language which they now call their own. The Spaniards and French likewise improved it into their respective tongues. From its great affinity to the Latin, it was called *Romance*, a name which the Spaniards still give to their own language. As the first legends of knight-errantry were written in Provencal, all subsequent performances of the same kind have derived from it the name of *romance;* and as those annals of chivalry contained extravagant adventures of knights, giants, and necromancers, every improbable story in fiction is to this day called a romance. Mr. Walpole, in his catalogue of royal and noble authors, has produced two songs in the ancient Provencal, written by our king Richard I. surnamed *Cœur de Lion;* and Voltaire, in his Historical Tracts, has favoured the world with some specimens of the same language. The *Patois* of Nice, must, without doubt, have undergone changes and corruptions in the course of so many ages, especially as no pains have been taken to preserve its original purity, either in orthography or pronunciation. It is neglected as the language of the vulgar; and scarce any body here knows either its origin or constitution. I have in vain endeavoured to procure some pieces in the ancient Provencal, that I might compare them with the modern *Patois*: but I can find no person to give me the least information on the subject. The shades of ignorance, sloth, and stupidity, are impenetrable. Almost every word of the *Patois* may still be found in the Italian, Spanish, and French languages, with a small change in the pronunciation. *Cavallo*, signifying a *horse* in Italian and Spanish, is called *cavao*; *maison*, the French word for a *house*, is changed into *maion*; *agua*, which means *water* in Spanish, the Niſſards call *daigua*. To express, *what a stop is here!* they say *acco fa lac aqui*, which is a a sentence composed of two Italian words, one French, and one Spanish. This is nearly the proportion in which these three languages will be found mingled in the *Patois* of Nice; which, with some variation, extends over all Provence, Languedoc, and Gascony. I will now treat you with two or three stanzas of a *canzon*, or hymn, in this language, to the Virgin Mary, which was lately printed at Nice.

I.	I.
Vierge, maire de Dieu,	Virgin mother of God,
Nuostro buono avocado,	Our good advocate,
Embel car uvostre fieu,	With your dear son,

LETTER XXI.

En Fenestro § audourado,	In Fenestro adored,
Jeu vous saludi,	I salute you,
E demandi en soccours;	And ask his assistance;
E senso autre preludi,	And without further prelude,
Canti lous uvostre honours.	I sing your honours.

2.

Qu' ario de Paradis!	What air of Paradise!
Que maesta divino!	What majesty divine!
Salamon es d' advis,	Solomon is of opinion,
Giugiar de uvostro mino;	To judge of your appearance;
Vous dis plus bello:	Says you are the fairest:
E lou dis ben soven	And it is often said
De toutoi lei femello,	Of all females,
E non s'engano ren.	And we are not at all deceived.

3.

Qu' airo de Paradis!	What air of Paradise!
Que maesta divino!	What majesty divine!
La bellezzo eblovis;	The beauty dazzles;
La bonta l'ueigl raffino.	The goodness purifies the eye:
Sias couronado,	You are crowned:
Tenes lou monde en man:	You hold the world in your
Sus del trono affettado,	Seated on the throne, [hands:
Riges lou uvostre enfan	You support your child.

You see I have not chosen this *canzon* for the beauty and elegance of thought and expression, but give it you as the only printed specimen I could find of the modern Provencal. If you have any curiosity to be further acquainted with the *Patois*, I will endeavour to procure you satisfaction. Meanwhile I am, in plain English, Dear Sir,

Ever yours.

§ *Fenestro is the name of a place in this neighbourhood, where there is a supposed miraculous sanctuary or chapel of the Virgin Mary.*

END OF VOLUME FIRST.

CPSIA information can be obtained
at www.ICGtesting.com
Printed in the USA
BVOW11s1118230418
514169BV00021B/1191/P